Praise for *The 10-Second Customer Journey*

Having led customer experience and overseen this critical business function, I have personally experienced the struggle of making an abstract topic concrete in different organizations. Todd turns decades of experience into practical advice with actionable approaches that anyone can understand. Finally!

Jeffrey J. Jones II, President and Chief Executive Officer of H&R Block, Former President Global Ride Sharing of Uber, Former Chief Marketing Officer of Target

In *The 10-Second Customer Journey*, Todd distills more than 30 years of marketing and digital experience into an actionable roadmap for driving growth in today's marketplace. More importantly, this book shows how seemingly unrelated parts of a career accumulate and layer on top of one another, until one day, they come together in a way that's perfect for the times. This is an excellent guide to modern-day marketing and customer experience and the role of the Chief Experience Officer in driving the future.

James Reed, Chairman and Chief Executive Officer of Reed and Author of **Life's Work, The 7-Second CV,** *and* **Why You?**

For brands and companies to grow, they will need to excel in every aspect of customer experience. This book illuminates what experience is in all its complexity. It shows how critical it is to remove friction in every part of the customer's journey, no matter where that journey begins or where it goes. A must-read for every business and business leader since you can't build a business without world-class customer experience. This is a primer on optimizing experience that is both actionable and inspiring.

Rishad Tobaccowala, Author of **Restoring the Soul of Business: Staying Human in the Age of Data**, *Former Chief Strategist of Publicis Groupe*

The 10-Second Customer Journey beautifully melds critical concepts that I have learned (often the hard way) over the course of a long career, with a few that are uniquely suited to help modern marketers navigate a complex, cluttered environment to grab all the customers they need. It's a great example of business writing that will be a mandatory read for my "Customer Empathy & Brand Experience Design" course at Duke, and I'm already putting it to great use counseling established and startup brands. True to its title, *The 10-Second Customer Journey* is a fast path to marketing excellence.

Brad Brinegar, Chairman Emeritus of McKinney and Executive In Residence at the Duke Innovation & Entrepreneurship Initiative

As CEO of the American Medical Association, I've seen firsthand the power of *The 10-Second Customer Journey* playbook in action. Todd's approach has transformed our growth trajectory, audience understanding, and digital platform. Even more, his growth-driven view of customer experience has increased teamwork and helped unify our mission and marketing initiatives. It's been instrumental in fulfilling our role as Physicians' Powerful Ally in Patient Care™.

James L. Madara, MD, Chief Executive Officer and Executive Vice President of the American Medical Association

Todd Unger connects the dots between old-school marketing know-how and modern digital-savvy power in this practical guide to reaching today's consumer. Useful, interesting, helpful... You will keep this book around for reference.

Donn Davis, Founder and Chairman of Professional Fighters League

Do you know how to convert browsers into customers in just ten seconds, and keep them for life? Todd compellingly argues that every 10-second customer interaction is a critical make-or-break experience. These moments define your relationship with customers, so handle them with the utmost care. Todd distills his decades of experience into a crisp playbook for executives and all customer-facing team members. From advice on "creating products that don't suck" to guidance on "developing a test-and-learn culture," this book is a treasure trove of hard-earned lessons. You owe it to your customers, and your business, to heed his advice.

Chunka Mui, Co-author of **A Brief History of a Perfect Future: Inventing the World We Can Proudly Leave Our Kids by 2050**

Over the years, I have observed hundreds, if not thousands, of people enter the realm of customer experience management with limited knowledge of how to adapt to and succeed in wrapping their arms around the discipline. Todd does a phenomenal job helping inform the scope and impact of getting introduced to this critical lifeline for true success. Great job pulling from real-life experience. Way to go, Todd! If you want to succeed, you'd better read!

Lou Carbone, Founder and Chief Executive Officer of Experience Engineering, Inc., and Professor at Michigan State University Broad School of Business

Disconnections across leadership, teams, and operations have always been a huge obstacle to great customer experience. As Todd points out in *The 10-Second Customer Journey*, today's split-second buying decisions make the stakes even higher. As one of the first Chief Customer Officers in the United States and an early leader in the field of customer experience (CX), I found the book's customer-first approach spot on. At its heart, Todd's playbook isn't just about technology, it's about integrating customer insight and technology to deliver your brand's promise. This book is indispensable reading for anyone working in or leading customer experience efforts today.

Jeanne Bliss, Author of **Chief Customer Officer 2.0** *and*
Co-founder of the Customer Experience
Professionals Association

The realities of today's digital economy are very challenging to navigate. There are constant changes in platforms, tools, regulations, and the introduction of trending mediums that require speculation and risk taking, such as the Metaverse and AI. Todd has had incredible success as a leader in marketing over decades, and his track record speaks for itself. *The 10-Second Customer Journey* breaks down how to remove the noise in the term "digital transformation" and focus on the core pillars and playbooks of growth marketing. This is a must-read not only for Chief Marketing Officers, but also for Chief Executive Officers and Chief Financial Officers so they can articulate strategies to their board, ask the right questions in leadership and management meetings, and be fluent in growth for the rising digital economy.

Reid Lappin, Founder and Chief Executive Officer of Vokal, a
Leading Growth Agency

Todd has drawn on his decades of senior corporate experience and enduring passion for customer excellence and re-writes the rules for customer experience in the split-second digital age. This groundbreaking book covers everything from outlining the critical role of Chief Experience Officers to developing a customer experience vison and detailed playbook for action. Finally, we have the guide we need to win the 10-second customer journey.

Claire O'Neill, Former UK Business Minister and Global Decarbonization Advisor

Marketing has become wildly complicated. This book turns complex tactics into a clear road map for action. Anyone managing a brand or company will benefit from the terrific frameworks and insights in this book.

Tim Calkins, Clinical Professor of Marketing at Kellogg School of Management, Northwestern University

In *The 10-Second Customer Journey*, Todd nails the importance of delivering frictionless experiences to grow any business. Even better, he delivers practical advice on how to do it well. A great read for marketers and management focused on exceptional customer experience.

Julia Fitzgerald, Chief Marketing Officer of Build-A-Bear and Author of the Best Seller **Midsize**

THE 10-SECOND CUSTOMER JOURNEY

The CXO's Playbook

for growing and retaining customers
in a digital world

TODD UNGER

First published in Great Britain by Practical Inspiration Publishing, 2024

ISBN   978-1-78860-590-8 (hardback)
       978-1-78860-503-8 (paperback)
       978-1-78860-505-2 (epub)
       978-1-78860-504-5 (mobi)

Want to bulk-buy copies of this book for your team and colleagues? We can customize the content and co-brand *The 10-Second Customer Journey* to suit your business's needs.

Please email info@practicalinspiration.com for more details.

Practical Inspiration
Publishing

Contents

Introduction

The internet changed customer experience forever. Buying decisions that used to take days or even months are now made in seconds. The tiniest delay, disconnect, or glitch in an interaction with a brand can send a potential customer packing. Yet more than 30 years after the public began going online, marketers, advertisers, and business owners are still playing catch-up.

Welcome to the world of the 10-second customer journey.

Maybe you think I'm exaggerating when I say "10-second," but think of the last time you ran across an ad on a website or on a social media platform that magically provided you with exactly what you were looking for, even if you didn't know you were looking for it. If the experience worked well, you clicked on the ad, read a little more about the product on a website, dropped it into a shopping cart, auto filled your payment information, and voilà, you were done in a few seconds.

A seamless, successful customer journey like the one I just described didn't happen by accident. Someone, or more correctly, some team, orchestrated that journey by deftly weaving together the four underlying elements of customer experience:

- **Marketing:** Serving you an ad with a relevant message that compelled you to act.

- **Product:** Offering you a solution that spoke to your needs and desires.
- **Commerce:** Making it lightning fast and painless for you to pay and be on your way.
- **Service:** Answering your questions along the way, so you didn't feel the need to delay, and eliminating potential trouble spots before they slowed you down.

Boom.

Now, think about the digital experiences you had recently, even today. Chances are that you didn't experience the 10-second customer journey. Maybe you were puzzled about why you even saw a certain ad. Maybe you clicked and didn't see what you were expecting. Or maybe like me, you were punished by a never-ending stream of captchas when you couldn't remember your password. Sometimes, don't you say to yourself, "OMG, I'm just trying to buy something from you!"

What is the enemy of the 10-second customer journey?

Friction.

Friction comes in many forms. We tend to think about friction as "mechanical" resistance or a breakdown – like a link that doesn't work on a web page, or an error when you hit "buy." But friction occurs before, during, and after the 10-second customer journey: An ad that seems irrelevant, instead of targeted; messaging that repels, instead of compels; a link to a page full of everything except the thing you wanted to see.

In this ever-changing digital landscape, organizations who can minimize friction, guiding potential buyers rapidly through the digital marketing buying process, will win.

Orchestrating a friction-free customer journey that cuts across both the digital and "real" worlds is a complex job by itself. But it's even more complicated because most organizations today are simply not aligned to deliver a seamless experience. With separate parts of the organization overseeing marketing, product development, (e-) commerce and customer service – and likely no one to lead them all together operationally – it's no wonder "getting to frictionless" seems nearly impossible. But there is a lot to gain by eliminating friction because it causes more than customer frustration and bad feelings. It prevents growth.

This book is about eliminating friction. Eliminate friction and you will drive growth.

One of the most important topics we will cover: Whose job is it to orchestrate a friction-free customer journey? Not surprisingly, the answer is often "everyone's." But the reality is that today's digital environment demands that organizations re-think their structures and recognize the need for a new kind of leader who drives growth by unifying marketing, product, commerce, and service. In the absence of that kind of organizational re-thinking, Chief Marketing Officers (CMO) often take the hit for organizations' inability to orchestrate a seamless customer journey. Without access to the full spectrum of customer experience levers – or perhaps only focused on limited portions of the customer journey (e.g., "branding") – CMOs face an uphill battle. Given the difficulty of driving growth in this environment, it is not surprising that the average tenure of today's CMOs, who are often held accountable for customer growth, has declined to roughly 40 months – its lowest level in a decade.[1] In an effort to re-ignite growth, companies often replace CMOs with new leaders, ones with titles like Chief Growth Officer (CGO) or Chief Customer Officer (CCO).

---

[1] Megan Graham, "Average CMO Tenure Holds Steady at Lowest Level in Decade" in *Wall Street Journal,* (2022, May 5). Available from: www.wsj.com/articles/average-cmo-tenure-holds-steady-at-lowest-level-in-decade-11651744800 [Accessed 13 February 2024].

Of course, replacing or adding different C-Suite leaders by itself is not going to work. The same organizational issues that prevent great customer experience just get passed on to someone new.

Customer experience is so important to customer growth that many companies have added another new C-Suite leader to the mix: Chief Experience Officer (CXO). While it is a relatively new C-Suite role, nearly 90% of U.S. companies have a CXO or equivalent role.[2] However, as I discovered, the job responsibilities and organizational structures are anything but well-defined.

As one of those CXOs who came to the role after a variety of marketing, product development, and digital commerce roles, I've seen firsthand the power of developing a new vision for customer experience in an organization. Because there wasn't a clearly defined road map for doing this, I've had to make it up myself to a certain extent, learning from customer experience pioneers and thought leaders, sewing together disparate pieces of my own multi-disciplinary experience, and experimenting with different ways of turning this knowledge into practice.

The 10-Second Customer Journey captures what I've learned so far about customer experience and the CXO role. It covers the building blocks of digital age customer experience and provides a playbook for translating this learning into a customer experience plan for your own brand or company. Whether you're a CXO, CXO-in-training, CMO, or a person who knows we can do better for customers by breaking free of traditional silos and re-aligning around growth, this book is for you.

---

[2] Stamford Conn, "Gartner Says Nearly 90% of Organizations Now Have a Chief Experience Officer or Chief Customer Officer or Equivalents" in Gartner, (2020, February 10). Available from: https://gartner.com/en/newsroom/press-releases/2020-02-10-gartner-says-nearly-90--of-organizations-now-have-a-c [Accessed 13 February 2024].

Here is a big picture outline of the ideas we will cover in the book:

- **Customer experience = growth.** While I'm a long-time marketer and digital executive, I'm a relatively newbie to the world of customer experience and the related discipline of "CX." It took me a while to connect all the dots between my experience and my role in driving customer growth as a CXO. In Chapters 1 and 2, we'll examine my journey, how I came to define the role of the CXO, and what a friction-free customer experience looks like.

- **Customer experience starts with the customer.** I know this may sound simplistic, but if we had a nickel for every failed initiative that started not with the customer, but with the product, we could stack them from here to Mars. That's why the first step in the playbook is about re-thinking your target audience in a way that paves the way for the 10-second customer journey.

- **The key to a great customer journey? Preparation.** You don't show up to a race expecting to run a four-minute mile. An achievement like that takes preparation. It's the same with the 10-second customer journey. You have to put in a lot of work before the clock even starts. As you'll see in Chapters 4, 5, and 6, that means having a digital-ready brand proposition, compelling product concept, and a well-developed storytelling platform.

- **Customer friction lives at the intersection of each step of the journey and beyond.** The slow-moving marketing funnel of yesterday has given way to a faster-moving "tornado funnel" where customers move through the buying process in seconds. But even the slightest amount of friction can bring things to a halt. The job of the CXO and the organization? Identify, predict, and eliminate friction at every stage. In Chapters 7, 8, and 9, we will look at how to avoid commerce-related friction through wide-scale testing and modern-day CX practices, so you can stop the endless "break-fix" cycle and fix the root causes of friction.

- **Technological change is inevitable. Make it work for you**. I've ridden every wave of digital transformation and leveraged the opportunities each one brought. New artificial intelligence (AI)-based technology, including generative learning models and analytics tools, represents the latest opportunity to build a friction-free future. Chapter 10 outlines the required mindset for future-facing leaders.

Before we dive into the playbook for the 10-second customer journey, I'll start with a little background about my own journey to the role of CXO. For one thing, I never set out to become a CXO. Frankly, before I was hired into the role seven years ago at the American Medical Association, I'm not certain I had ever even heard of the title.

I had a lot to learn.

The journey begins

Chapter 1
The accidental CXO

When I first became the CXO of the American Medical Association (AMA), I got a lot of questions. "What does customer experience mean?", "Is customer experience the same thing as customer service?", "What does a Chief Experience Officer do?" My favorite comment came from former U.S. Surgeon General Jerome Adams, who told me I had a cool title. I said I'd be willing to trade with him (his uniform was way cooler).

I understood what the AMA was looking for me to do, which was to grow our membership base, but others were clearly unsure. To come up with some better answers to the types of questions I was getting, and to make sure I had a clear vision of the role, I decided to do some research.

I am not above Googling my title to figure this out. Don't tell anyone, but that's exactly what I did when I became a Chief Digital Officer (CDO) years before. I typed "What is customer experience?" and "What does a Chief Experience Officer do?" into my search bar. I expected to find a complete answer and clear description of my job responsibilities. Instead, I just had a lot more questions. For an idea that has its roots in marketing, the term "customer experience" could really use a brand repositioning. I was surprised by the vagueness of "customer experience" definitions and the overall lack of clarity about the CXO role. Some online entries explained customer experience as literally anything that affected customer perceptions of the brand, which is very broad. Others viewed customer experience primarily in terms of customer service, focused on the efficiency and technology of call centers, which was too narrow. Still others saw customer experience rooted in "user experience," a concept out of the design world, which didn't feel relevant.

Most definitions of customer experience applied to live and in-person experiences or customer service interactions that generally occur after purchase. But in today's digitally driven world, customer experience is not about a "place." It is just as likely to occur on a website, a social media platform, or even through email. And it begins the moment a potential customer demonstrates even the smallest spark of interest, not just after they buy something.

Since I couldn't find a clear definition of customer experience, I wasn't surprised that I couldn't find a clear definition of the CXO role either. The job responsibilities I found were equally vague and varied, either too broad or narrow. Some definitions were more rooted in important leadership qualities like "being collaborative with other executives" rather than specific guidance about the job to be done. None of them focused on growth.

Since there was no clear road map for the role as I saw it – one focused on customer growth – I realized I was going to have to make one up myself. To do that, I needed to develop a good working definition of "customer experience" and then build a succinct explanation of what a CXO does to drive it. This book charts my journey and what I've learned along the way about how to grow and retain customers in a digital world.

***

I am always intrigued by the celebrated accounts of high-profile designers who take over storied fashion brands. The first thing they often do is go back to the archives, looking for the essence of the brand from its historic roots and past designs. I took a page from that metaphorical book. Before I looked ahead to define the role of the CXO in the digital age, I looked back at the roots and history of customer experience to understand its essence. Where did the term "customer experience" come from? When did it morph into its shorter form, "CX"?

In its earliest conception, customer experience grew out of academic discussions of "experiential consumption," a term to describe the set of sensory perceptions and feelings that surround the use of products and services.[1] But the term "customer experience" and its arrival as a field of marketing study and focus are credited to Lewis Carbone, who wrote the 1994 Marketing and Management article with Stephan Haeckel entitled "Engineering Customer Experiences." Carbone and Haeckel defined customer experience as "the 'take-away' impression formed by people's encounters with products, services and businesses – a perception produced when humans consolidate sensory information."[2]

Carbone and Haeckel's work launched an entirely new way of thinking about what people were buying when they became customers. In their groundbreaking article, as well as in subsequent publications, Carbone and Haeckel laid out the need for organizations to deliver and compete on "experiences"

---

[1] Brian Lofman, "Elements of Experiential Consumption: An Exploratory Study" in NA – *Advances in Consumer Research*, 18, (1991) and Hirschman and Holbrook's Thought-Emotion-Activity-Value (TEAV) Model (1986).

[2] Lewis P. Carbone and Stephan H. Haeckel, "Engineering Customer Experiences" in *Marketing Management*, 3 (3), (1994, January).

by orchestrating a set of cues that consumers consciously or subconsciously pick up on during the buying process.

In other words, customers aren't just buying a product. They're buying an experience. That terminology rang a bell because it was a transformative and highly publicized marketing idea in its time. In other words, customer experience was the secret sauce that the most successful companies added to distinguish their offerings and create loyalty. Whether it was the cleanliness and uniformity of McDonald's or the attention to detail at Walt Disney World, these customer experience elements created both distinctiveness and loyalty.

To have the right secret sauce, companies first had to "gain an understanding of the customer's journey – from the expectations they have before the experience occurs to the assessments they are likely to make when it's over."[3] This quote undoubtedly launched a million *customer journey maps*.

When Berry, Carbone, and Haeckel wrote in 2002 about the need to understand the customer journey, the concept at the time still focused on in-person, live interactions. But at that moment, everything was about to change. The internet and the advent of digital marketing and e-commerce dramatically altered the paradigm of experience. The arrival of the internet didn't make customer experience obsolete by any means, but it necessitated a broader definition to encompass an entirely new set of challenges.

Around the same time as Carbone and Haeckel's original article, Don Peppers and Martha Rogers added a complementary dimension to the concept of customer experience with their

---

[3] Leonard L. Berry, Lewis P. Carbone, and Stephan H. Haeckel, "Managing the Total Customer Experience" in *MIT Sloan Management Review*, (2022, April 15). Available from: https://sloanreview.mit.edu/article/managing-the-total-customer-experience/ [Accessed 13 February 2024].

book, *The One to One Future*. They painted a vision of personalized marketing communication based on newly powerful databases and developing "interactive" (the old word for digital) technologies. Given the timing, Peppers' and Rogers' book was both revolutionary and downright visionary. Underlying their vision of personalization was a new way of thinking about customers through data-driven segmentation, with an objective of identifying core "heavy users" and nurturing direct relationships with them.

Over the next decade, the original paradigm of customer experience transitioned into the more formalized and distinct discipline called "customer experience" (CX). CX pioneers like Jeanne Bliss, one of the original CCOs, and Bruce Temkin, a former analyst at Forrester and former Head of the Qualtrics XM Institute, began developing frameworks around enterprise CX capabilities, focusing on measuring customer perceptions, and tying these to business outcomes. One of Temkin's key tenets is that CX reflects a company's culture and organizational processes, not just its technology.

Subsequently, there has been an "X"-plosion of other types of experience, with UX (user experience), DX (digital experience), MX (multi-platform experience), EX (employee experience), and even XM (experience management). Technology vendors often position customer service tools as CX platforms. In general, the terms "customer experience" and "CX" are often bandied about interchangeably, but somehow in the transition from the big idea of customer experience to discipline of CX, a lot more changed than just a bunch of letters.

No wonder I was confused. I found it very difficult to process a definition of customer experience that literally encompassed every customer interaction across every possible touchpoint over time eternity. I needed a working definition of experience that went beyond that of live experiences and considered more than just customer perceptions and feelings. A definition that was about driving growth and retaining customers in a digital world.

Rest assured I did not sit around waiting to figure this out before I did my job at AMA. But after three years, it came to me – a practical definition that described what I was doing and how I was leading:

> *Customer experience is the seamless integration of product, marketing, commerce, and service to acquire and retain customers.*

On my third anniversary at the AMA, I shared this definition on LinkedIn to mark the occasion. I received a fair amount of positive feedback, but I also got some pushback because my definition of customer experience did not incorporate anything about feelings. "How can you focus on customer experience without paying attention to what the customers are feeling?" someone asked.

I get it. How customers feel is important to the outcome. But it's not enough. As a growth leader, I found several practical limitations when focusing on feelings:

- Feelings are hard to quantify.
- Feelings are not necessarily insightful, actionable, or effective for fixing problems.
- Feelings are intermediary and therefore difficult to associate directly with business growth and return on investment.
- If you can't associate feelings directly to growth and ROI, then it's very hard to get people to invest in them.
- Much of traditional CX is oriented around how people interpret and feel about live interactions. It is a lot harder to apply those principles when the experience is mostly, if not all, digital.

With my growth-focused definition in place, I had a charted path for my role as CXO. I now began to look at my responsibilities through a different lens. I even began to look at my title differently. My job was about more than just increasing our membership base.

It was up to me to seamlessly integrate our product, marketing, commerce, and service.

My job was to put the "X" in CXO.

The "X" in CXO is the intersection between the customer (C) and the organization (O). The four corners of the X are the core components of customer experience – marketing, product, commerce, and service. These four components, when brought together, create a single, unified customer experience model that drives growth.

With that realization, I had a guide on how to move forward. It was time for me to start putting the "X" in CXO and talking to others inside and outside my organization about the same approach.

In retrospect, the "putting the X in CXO" approach wasn't exactly random. Unknowingly, I had gone back to the archives – on myself. Each element in the customer experience definition I came up with corresponded to different chapters of my career. Paraphrasing organizational scholar Karl Weick, we make sense of our experiences and lives retrospectively. When I looked back on my career, I realized there were four distinct phases that uniquely corresponded to the four building blocks of customer experience I had laid out in my definition:

- **Marketing**: I worked in brand management at Procter & Gamble (P&G) and advertising at the Leo Burnett Company, where I learned the fundamentals of customer segmentation and brand proposition, marketing strategy and planning, advertising strategy and creative production, and consumer product development. This is where I learned how to champion the customer and to translate consumer needs into new products and marketing initiatives.

- **Product**: The next steps in my career focused on digital product development, content management and packaging, and digital website management at AOL, Time Inc., Lifetime Television, and several digital gaming startups. This is where I learned to translate consumer needs into digital products, how to get digital products built, and how to grow digital audience.

- **Commerce**: I spent more than six years as the CMO and CDO at the *Daily Racing Form*, a long-established print media company in horse racing that moved into data subscription services, premium digital content, and a digital betting platform. My role was to drive customer growth with digital platforms, attracting potential customers through content, digital advertising, and social media and then converting them into customers across the breadth of our offerings. A huge part of "customer experience" came from analyzing commerce flows to eliminate friction and optimizing the buying experience through constant testing.

- **Service**: In addition to overseeing membership and brand marketing at the AMA, my team also includes a consolidated customer service center that supports the entire organization. It was the first time I'd ever taken on responsibility for a customer service operation, and I approached it with an appreciation for the rigors and metrics of a well-run operation. But as a newcomer to the world of customer service, I also had an outsider's perspective on the impact customer service could have beyond solving immediate customer problems.

For me, this last phase of my career is where it all came together – the four major building blocks of customer experience: Marketing, product, commerce, and service.

Now, I know what you're thinking: *Are you telling me I need to spend 30 years across multiple disciplines and jobs to become a CXO or CX leader?* Nope. I had to blunder my way through this process with no guide. You can hopefully shave a couple of decades off the journey by reading this book and learning how to orchestrate the elements of a digital era customer experience.

You also might wonder: *Why does marketing come first in your customer experience definition?* Well, for a couple of reasons. First, as you'll see in the playbook portion of the book, a lot of the "up-front" work of customer experience – starting with customer definition and brand strategy – has a marketing focus.

Second, I'm probably biased by having much of my past training and current focus on marketing. There is some temptation for me to think about the CXO role as "CMO +" because of the interconnected responsibilities required to create and retain customers in this environment. But being a CXO is more than about marketing – it's about aligning the organization around customer growth. As disciplines, the worlds of marketing and customer experience are like lost organizational soulmates. Once joined, they can begin to transform even the stodgiest corporations and help turn them into growth machines.

While my definition of customer experience may be different than others, at least it is a reasonable stake in the ground. The field of customer experience is still formative, and companies' appetite for growth never stops. While many organizations have a CXO or equivalent role, the job responsibilities and organizational structures vary greatly. Some CXOs focus primarily on customer service, while others zero in on operations, marketing, or retail experience. It may be some time before a more uniform job description emerges, but what is becoming increasingly clear is that orchestrating customer experience is a high-level job that requires cross-disciplinary operational authority and collaboration to make real change.

Title is not really the issue though. Customer experience in the digital age is about a new kind of leadership and organizational approach that meets the needs of today's customers. Will the field of customer experience continue to thrive as a distinct discipline with a defined leader like the CXO to drive it forward? That remains to be seen. Fifteen or twenty years ago, when "digital transformation" was the hot topic, organizations rushed to hire CDOs like me to help chart out new territory. But over time, these same organizations began building new digital muscles and incorporating them in different ways. The roles and responsibilities that were once so acutely necessary got absorbed as digital transformation became the new normal.

In that regard, I found this headline from a Forbes.com article to be quite accurate: "The CXO title may be temporary, but the role will be permanent."[4]

---

[4] Olof Schybergson, "The CXO Title May Be Temporary, But the Role Will Be Permanent" in *Forbes*, (2021, August 23). Available from: www.forbes.com/sites/forbesagencycouncil/2021/08/23/the-cxo-title-may-be-temporary-but-the-role-will-be-permanent/?sh=2016a 565109b [Accessed 13 February 2024].

Chapter 2
The need for speed

The original concept of customer experience was rooted in live experiences and "sensory cues." But what does the concept of customer experience mean in the digital age, when there is an entirely different set of sensory cues and no physical environment at all? What does the "seamless integration of marketing, product, commerce, and service" look like in a digital world?

And why is this so darn hard to pull off?

I thought back to an earlier online buying experience that had a big impact on how I thought about the meaning of "seamless integration." It involved a customer journey – to France. I'm not sure what it is like in your family, but in mine (especially when my kids were young), I had another role: Chief Travel Planner. Several years ago, I was tasked with planning our family's spring break trip. Once we had narrowed down our desired location to Paris, I went to work, doing what millions of people do every day: I turned to the internet.

I typed in "Best family vacation ideas Paris."

That's the equivalent of sending up red flares in the digital ecosystem, unleashing the travel industry advertising Kraken.

In this case, it wasn't a monster I was unleashing, but a set of responses competing for my next click. I chose one that said something like "fast, easy travel packages to Paris." This took me to a page on a major travel site – not the home page, but a special destination that walked me through the process of planning the trip to Paris. Within a few minutes of my first click, I had selected my flights, picked a hotel, and dropped a chunk of money on the trip. But with my air and travel reservations locked down, I could focus on the rest of the upcoming journey itself.

I've reflected on this customer experience many times since. Like so many effective customer journeys, I didn't think about what it required on the other end to put together that seamless interaction. But, of course, someone was prepared to see the flares that I sent up. Someone chose to deliver the ad that caught my attention (targeting). Someone had to think about what I saw next when I clicked, and what words or images would entice me to continue (marketing). Someone had to pull all the elements of the travel package together, so it was easy for me to make choices without stopping to think, *I'd better do more research* (product, service). And someone had to build a commerce path and engine that allowed me to turn all those selections into a purchase in a matter of minutes (commerce).

I had just experienced what I now call "the 10-second customer journey."

This same 10-second customer journey plays itself out millions of times every day, with decisions large and small. Done right, this process compresses the time between the vaguest notion of "I want something" to "I search for something" to "I see something" to "I bought something" from months and days to minutes and seconds. And with the advent of new AI-powered search technologies, where the prompt "help me plan my vacation" is answered not with a set of websites, but with a complete itinerary, things are about to move even faster.

The 10-second customer journey, with its whole-system view of customer experience – blending marketing, product, commerce, and service – became a touchstone for me as I contemplated my role as a CXO. In fact, I'd say as a CXO today, my primary role as a leader is orchestrating the 10-second journey for customers, helping my team and colleagues work to drive growth in a way unlike we – or any business – had to do before.

Now, I hear the skeptics saying sarcastically, "Wow, the internet made things go faster, that's so profound." But the real significance of the 10-second customer journey is not just the speed at which experiences now occur, but also when and how they occur. As we contemplate the new, faster customer journey, it is helpful to examine how we used to think about it not so long ago. The basic concept here is one that every student learns about in their first marketing class. It is called the "marketing funnel."

The marketing funnel has been a fundamental marketing model since its conception in 1898 by Elias St. Elmo Lewis.[1] The funnel metaphor provided a framework for consumer and business-to-business marketers as they guided prospective customers from awareness to interest, from interest to desire, and from desire to purchase.

Traditionally, marketers envisioned this process as sequential, with specific marketing activities deployed within different layers of the funnel to move a potential customer from "I see it" to "I love it." At the top of the funnel, marketers focused on building "brand awareness" with enormous television and print budgets. In the middle of the funnel, marketers piqued consumers' interest and desire with additional information and claims, moving them through the consideration stage. At the bottom of the funnel,

---

[1] E. K. Strong, Jr. *The Psychology of Selling and Advertising.* New York, p. 9 and p. 349 (1925).

spurred by their research and evaluation, the consumer buys the product, often with the aid of a trial incentive like a coupon or other special promotions. Finally, based on their experience with the product, the consumer would decide whether to buy again.

This funnel process provided the framework for customer experience for the better part of a century. The funnel did not include customer service – then considered the department where consumers called for more information or with complaints and feedback about the product. The main job of marketers in this paradigm was to create desire, or the sense of "I want it." Once the marketer successfully created desire, the consumer would purchase the product in a retail setting.

The internet ended this paradigm abruptly.

Powered by their newfound ability to research, discover, compare, and communicate, consumers no longer move gingerly and sequentially through the marketing funnel. This new era, made possible by the "red flares" of the digital ecosystem and a bevy of new websites, social platforms, and algorithms, allows for an entirely new and compressed customer experience, where consumers speed rapidly, and sometimes simultaneously, through the stages of awareness, interest, desire, and action. The concept of service is no longer limited to the end but is pervasive throughout the funnel. And, of course, in a digital world, the buying experience often circumvents the traditional retail environment altogether or relegates it to a pickup.

Goodbye, slow-moving marketing funnel. Hello, "tornado funnel."

I call it the "tornado funnel" because the traditional funnel has been tossed in the air and whipped around, mixing the individual steps in the customer journey together and mashing it all into a new customer experience. One that is rapid. One that is unpredictable. And one that is constantly changing.

Managing the tornado funnel is about creating a fluid funnel experience and painstakingly removing all obstacles for consumers across all platforms, especially mobile. That is a tough ask for any organization, but the shift has been an especially difficult challenge to legacy organizations bound by old-school silos that each carry responsibility for certain aspects of the customer journey.

Imagine you're in charge of customer growth, but you have basically no control or influence over product development, the digital commerce infrastructure, or customer service. Maybe all those different areas have incentives that don't exactly align with yours. Maybe your purview is limited to brand strategy and advertising while the mechanics of creative development and placement, digital strategy, social media, analytics, and customer segmentation are spread out over a plethora of departments and external agencies. This is basically life for many CMOs today. They simply lack the levers, mandate, and even perhaps the experience to drive growth in a landscape entirely transformed by digital. Leading in these conditions is like trying to exist happily and find success in the middle of a tornado.

I've seen this organizational situation many times before in my career; first as an account executive at an advertising agency, where there was a wall between the creative (product) and business (marketing) sides, and later, as a digital executive at a traditional magazine publishing firm where I ran into the hard, "church and state" wall between the editorial staff (product) and the business side (sales and marketing). The advent of digital platforms, publishing, and marketing laid waste to these divides, yet countless businesses are still stuck with these walls and silos.

In this new era, organizations need to get it together. They need leaders who can help tame the tornado funnel and make the 10-second customer journey a reality. That's where the CXO comes in.

Driving growth in the digital world is no longer just about creating desire and then handing off the customer to another department to close the deal. Driving growth today is about connecting all the elements (marketing, product, commerce, and service) that turn a prospect into a customer in seconds. This is a useful way to think about the difference between the traditional CMO model and today's CXO role. A CMO's focus is on "I want it" and creating desire, while a CXO thinks through the entire process, igniting desire and removing the friction along the path toward "I got it," and hopefully, "I love it."

The CXO is a full tornado funnel expert, responsible for harnessing the power of the digital winds that drive a consumer from "I see it" to "I love it." No longer limited to the top of the funnel, the CXO plays a role throughout the process, eliminating friction at every stage and unifying the customer experience.

Now it's time to enter the playbook section of the book. In the coming chapters, I'll share the steps you can take to tame the tornado funnel and orchestrate the 10-second customer journey. You might be surprised about the first step. It is often the one that people skip, introducing friction from the start.

The playbook

Chapter 3
Customer experience starts with the customer

The first step to orchestrating the 10-second customer journey happens before the clock even starts. To borrow an overused term, you can't be "customer-centric" unless you start with the customer.

Unless you've determined your target audience properly up front – based on data – your journey will be starting with friction. It's the marketing equivalent of throwing sand in the gears from the get-go. To use Monopoly game terminology, until you've completed this first step, do not pass go. In fact, don't even think about rolling the dice.

When I reflect on my own career, every major business advance I made began with challenging assumptions about the customer or target audience definition. Conversely, most of the mistakes I made happened because I started instead with what I thought was a great new product idea.

This chapter will cover the key techniques I've learned about defining and articulating the target audience and leveraging this understanding to drive growth.

***

Let me say it again for emphasis: *Defining the target customer remains the first and most important step in customer experience.* This is even more important in a digital environment, where target inputs such as online behavior, attitudes, and usage are essential to reaching the right audience and driving conversion.

Do you work in an organization or business where everyone can clearly describe the target customers for the company's products or services? In my experience, many don't. Why is that? Put simply, many of the "old-school" tools of the consumer marketing and advertising world, particularly customer segmentation, got left in the dust as we moved into the digital world.

At many companies, it is not unusual to have the target customer be assumed or described in overly broad brushstrokes that provide little actionable intelligence. You'll sometimes even hear the marketing kiss of death: "Our target audience is everyone!" Other times, you'll be handed demographic data such as "Women aged 25 to 54" or be introduced to "Pete, the fake customer persona," a hypothetical character developed to bring the customer to life for people across the company when they discuss new business ideas.

Even worse than fake personas are what I call "aspirational targets" that define an attractive customer segment but aren't connected to data. A friend called me last year with a story just like this. Their agency had defined the ideal target customer for a new spirits brand to be a young, fun-loving, social media-savvy woman who was interested in social justice issues and the like. While hypothetically this might seem like an attractive target customer – affluent, nightlife-oriented – there was just one problem. When I asked him what data this characterization was based on, the answer was "None." In other words, there was no real evidence to suggest that these audience qualities would translate into preference for their type or brand of liquor.

In my experience, the tendency to skip over the customer definition step is particularly prevalent in the digital world. Many digitally oriented companies I've worked for tended to be a bit of the Wild West when it came to consumer marketing, moving from one emergency to another. Like tech companies before them, digital companies also tend to be very product-first operations.

Granted, there are certainly examples of product and service innovations that started with a product idea. The iPhone. Wrinkle-free pants. Beanie Babies. But there are a million examples of failed product ideas that never found an audience.

***

You might not have thought about target audience definition as the first step in customer experience. But in today's digital world, you can leverage an actionable target definition in ways I never could have imagined when I first started my career. By using data to identify the *current* behaviors and attitudes that predict *future* behavior, you'll know how to reach your target and how big your target audience is.

The technical marketing term for the process of identifying your customer is "target segmentation." Simply put, it's a data-driven approach to separating the customers you are going after from everyone else. The target segmentation process involves some kind of quantitative research. The process may involve an outside research firm that specializes in this field, but as you will see, it is possible to do a lot on your own.

There are a million different ways to segment potential customers. The objective is to develop a segmentation that predicts who is more likely to purchase your product than other people. For example, I could separate out all the brown-eyed people or all the people 40 years or older from the rest of the population. That kind of segmentation is unlikely to predict anything about these customers' desire to buy anything. On the other hand, I could separate "fitness enthusiasts" from the crowd. Knowing someone is a fitness enthusiast would predict their interest in fitness apparel or a gym membership relative to everyone else.

Designing great segmentation research – the kind that yields actionable insight – is an art *and* a science. And because I haven't always had access to a research firm for help, I've learned to be scrappy and design these studies on my own.

To create an effective target segmentation, you need to see customers in "4-D."

Seeing customers in 4-D means collecting *four* specific types of data to help understand who your high-potential customer segments are, and just as important, who won't be part of your target audience. You can use this approach in just about any type of segmentation research, from scrappy to pricey.

Here are the four kinds of data you need to get a 4-D view:

1. **Behavioral**: Here's one of the key pieces of targeting wisdom I learned at Leo Burnett: *The best predictor of future behavior is current behavior.* Behavioral data helps you identify what your potential customers are already doing that could drive interest in your business or a new product idea. I'm not saying that it is impossible for someone to adopt a new behavior. For instance, I might decide to prioritize fitness and start running three days a week. This behavior change would cause me to be interested in high-end running shoes. But if your product requires me to change my behavior, that's a much harder sell. At my age, you're just not going to convince me to drink your brand of milk if I don't drink milk to begin with.

2. **Attitudinal**: Understanding how customers think and feel can provide a powerful basis for segmentation on its own or in combination with behaviors. The fancy term for this is "psychographic characteristics," but I tend to think about them more simply as "attitudes." For example, there are a million different brands of fitness attire. Which one I pick has as much to do with how I think about myself and attitudes about fitness as it does with the substantive qualities of the shirt or shorts. For example, if I am not confident about my body when I work out, I will probably stick with a crew neck t-shirt instead of a sleeveless "muscle shirt." My preference could change if I become more buff, but the brand that meets me where I am now is the one I'm more likely to choose.

3. **Product concept**: Once you've collected a good amount of data about various customers' behaviors and attitudes, you're ready to show them some product ideas to get their opinions – usually on a five-point scale, from "definitely interested" to "definitely not interested." The biggest mistake people make is rushing to this step without having adequate information from the first two steps. Without the behavioral and attitudinal information, it's hard to determine why some people are "very interested" in a product concept, while others have no interest at all.

4. **Demographics**: You should absolutely capture key data around age, gender, income, location, etc. Demographic data can provide additional clues or distinctions between segments and important targeting data. But demographic characteristics alone are rarely the primary driver of purchase decisions. For example, let's say your product is a high-end, limited-edition sneaker. If you were to segment the sneaker buyer market, you could probably pinpoint the type of person who collects shoes like these. More than likely, the demographics of this group would

be young and male. So, now you have a target of "sneaker collector" + young + male to work with. But if you just started with demographics only, say, just the "young + male" part, you would be including a lot of folks who have no interest whatsoever in your product.

***

With those data elements in hand, let's talk about an example that shows how you can use the 4-D model to segment the market and get a sense of just how large your target audience is. We'll start with a scrappy segmentation study that I did myself at the *Daily Racing Form*.

For those who aren't familiar with horse racing, it was once the largest spectator sport in the United States. The *Daily Racing Form*, often called DRF or just "The Form," is like the *New York Times* of horse racing. If you've ever been to a horse race, you've likely seen folks in the stands clutching "The Form" and poring over the hieroglyphic-like statistics on every page that inform their betting strategies. The process of using data to inform betting decisions is called "handicapping."

Founded as a tabloid newspaper in Chicago by Frank Brunell in 1894, the *Daily Racing Form* remains the authoritative source on horse racing, providing news and data to racing enthusiasts (called horseplayers) throughout the United States and Canada. Today, it has evolved from its newspaper roots into a full-fledged digital platform. A big part of my job as CMO and CDO was expanding the reach of its digital content, creating more data customers, and launching an online betting platform.

At one point, we were considering offering a premium content tier and putting certain digital content for serious horseplayers behind a subscriber paywall. To size up this opportunity and design our approach, we needed to answer two important questions: "Who exactly is the target audience?" and "How big is the market for this?"

For some, the target audience was "all horseplayers," the equine equivalent of the marketing kiss of death, as that was literally the equivalent of "everyone" in our world. I had a feeling our target audience was much more specific, but I needed the data to prove it. Instead of heading to the track to talk to players, I used a popular and inexpensive online survey tool to help me develop the appropriate segmentation. To my surprise, more than 1,000 players responded.

Here is how I used the 4-D target segmentation model to answer our key questions:

1. **Behavioral**: I started by identifying existing behaviors that might help predict future behavior. In this case, I was looking for the kinds of behavior that would drive interest in a premium content product. For horse racing, behavioral data meant things like:

    a. How many times did the customer visit our website?
    b. How much did they spend on racing data?
    c. How often did they visit a racetrack?
    d. Did they have an online betting account?
    e. How often and how much did they bet on horses at the racetrack or online?

    In addition to these "close-in" type behavioral questions, you can expand into related behavioral areas to identify other potential drivers. For instance, in this research, we could have asked about customers' other habits such as sports and casino betting.

2. **Attitudinal**: This part was about capturing beliefs and feelings that might separate the target audience from others. In the case of the *Daily Racing Form*, we asked how our customers felt about the quality of our content relative to other sources, how confident they felt about betting with certain handicapping tools, and their beliefs and attitudes about risk. But there are all kinds of

attitudinal data that may be relevant to your segmentation and prediction of future behavior, including political beliefs or even perceptions about success.

3. **Product concept**: With the foundation of behavioral and attitudinal questions in place, we then asked all the respondents about their level of interest in our premium content idea. On the 5-point scale, we were looking for those who chose "4" (probably interested) or "5" (definitely interested), otherwise known as the "Top 2 Box."

4. **Demographics**: Again, and I apologize in advance for the bad pun, we didn't put the cart before the horse here. Horse racing is already a very niche sport, and many of the participants are older, male, and with at least enough disposable income to bet. We didn't expect to see anything significant here, but the data would tell.

Once the survey was complete with plenty of responses, we looked at the four types of data to see what stood out. I was able to use the survey software to identify a *combination* of three factors that distinguished a high-potential audience for the premium content offering:

- **Behavior**: Visited the Daily Racing Form.com site more than three times a week.

- **Attitude**: Felt the news and information from the *Daily Racing Form* was superior to other sources of horse racing information.

- **Behavior**: Had an online betting account.

Now, trust me. I hear you saying, "You went to all the trouble to learn *that?*" And on the surface, it all seems commonsensical, right?

But was this the hypothetical target audience of "everyone?" Not at all. This group represented only about 5% of all the horseplayers who responded to the survey. This was a small segment, but as the research showed us, potentially valuable to our marketing and product development (and note, nowhere in that target audience description was there anything about these folks' age, gender, or location).

Had we gone with the "all horseplayers" theory, we would have wasted precious time and even more precious marketing dollars pitching a service that didn't appeal to 95% of players. Not only would we not have generated revenue from them, but we also would have annoyed them with repetitive messages promoting a service the research showed they were highly unlikely to ever try.

The research also gave us a much better sense of just how big a revenue opportunity there might be for a premium content offering. This was important since there were both risks and costs associated with putting up a paywall on a formerly free site.

This segmentation was scrappy, but it was grounded in data, not guesswork. We didn't assume that "everyone is the target," or create "fake" customer personas that attempted to approximate a target description without the actionable 4-D customer view.

While not transformative, the *Daily Racing Form* research provides a tactical example of how target segmentation – customer identification if you will – can inform your business strategy. But over the years, I've also done target segmentation research that literally changed the course of the businesses I was working on. This research varied in sophistication and cost, and each used the tools available at the time, but they all provided the kind of insight that creates a "customer-centric" foundation. The one common trait? They were all based on data that reflected what these customers did, bought, and believed.

Let's take a look at two variations from two very different audiences that I've worked with: plastic zipper bag buyers and, in my current role, physicians.

Plastic zipper bags: Find the heavy users

The first segmentation study I ever did was in the not-very-sexy but still interesting world of plastic zipper bags. These are the kind of plastic food storage bags that you can seal at the top. The brand that I worked on at the time was called Glad-Lock. It was known for its "yellow and blue make green" seal technology, which indicated that the bag was securely closed.

Prior to my starting in the Glad-Lock business, the target segmentation model was demographic. The segmentation model differentiated the buyers of three bag types based on age, income, and location characteristics:

- Sandwich bag users = younger, lower income

- Food storage bag users = families, Northeastern skew

- Freezer bag users = older, Southern skew

We bought millions of dollars of television and print media ads based on these demographic descriptions, switching between target audiences over the course of the year in line with seasonal consumption patterns.

But there was something that didn't seem very "fresh" about this segmentation to me.

The biggest red flag was the demographic differences between customer segments weren't exactly overwhelming. The variations were a few percentage points, at best. It seemed to me that there wasn't any defining demographic characteristic that accounted for one person using one bag type over another.

So, one day, I scratched down on a piece of paper three overlapping circles, one for each bag type customer:

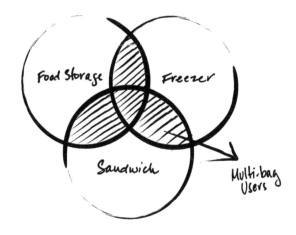

My thought was that by analyzing different parts of the circles, we might see something interesting. At the time, there was no such thing as digital commerce data. What we did have was "panel data." Talk about a non-digital world! The panel data literally came from information provided by consumers who filled out a daily diary on paper about what and how much they used across a wide variety of products. This information included not only their product purchases, but also a lot of other information about their media habits and hobbies.

It was kind of like an old-fashioned, pre-digital version of the 4-D research model. That was good enough at the time.

When we analyzed usage against this new overlapping circle framework, something very interesting became apparent. Consumers who fell into the overlapping areas – those who said they used multiple types of bags – represented less than 20% of the total buyer population but more than 75% of consumption of all bags. What about the group in the very middle who used all three bag types? They were about 10% of customers who represented almost 60% of bag consumption! We called these two groups "multi-bag users" and "heavy multi-bag users." This target description was about as sexy as the plastic bag category, but it turned out to be very actionable.

What distinguished "multi-bag users" from others (beyond the sheer number of bags they consumed) were the associated behaviors that drove the consumption. These folks were off the charts on their interest in cooking, gardening, looking at recipes, and reading shelter magazines. It turned out that plastic bag consumption wasn't being driven by age, income, or region at all. It was all about behavior: Consumers with a lot of food preparation and cooking-related behaviors needed a lot of food storage bags.

This was a world before digital targeting capabilities, but the data was very actionable, even for "old media." We immediately shifted our approach to media planning and promotion, using the new behavioral target definition for buying media. Since our budget exceeded $10 million dollars, more efficient, targeted media buying was a huge win. But in addition, this new understanding of our target audience changed our view on how we went about evaluating new product ideas.

Remember the steps earlier in this chapter: Discover the underlying behaviors and attitudes first, *then* test product concepts. By skipping the first steps, it turned out we had been talking to the wrong people about a new product idea, with potentially serious consequences.

As part of a new product development initiative, I'd come up with an idea for a reusable, dishwasher-safe plastic container, an alternative to more expensive containers. Initial focus group reactions among the demographic-based, general plastic bag user audience were unimpressive. Based on the new target segmentation, I pressed to re-do the focus group research using our redefined target – the "multi-bag" users.

This seemed a bit of a waste of time to the somewhat crusty research director. But the results were completely different and highly favorable. The plastic container concept became the highest-scoring new product idea in our agency's history. A year later, GladWare plastic containers hit store shelves and were a huge success.

Here's the bottom line: Knowing who your target audience is – and isn't – can lead to immediate improvements in how you reach your customers. But better target segmentation can also provide more accurate direction for driving product innovation.

Now, let's flash forward almost (eek) 25 years, where I'm still going strong with my target segmentation approach. At this point in digital history, we don't need to rely on customers reporting their activities in paper diaries. We have a new "digital paper trail" to follow. But while technology made it easier to get the data, the principles underpinning the segmentation approach stayed the same.

Physicians: Increasing engagement with targeted content

Founded in 1847, the AMA is the largest and only national association in the United States that convenes nearly 200 state and specialty medical societies and other critical stakeholders. The association represents the nation's 1.5 million physicians, resident physicians, and medical students in their efforts to improve patient care.

When I first arrived at the AMA, the predominant audience segmentation was logical and career-based: Medical students, residents, and physicians. These career stages are obviously important distinctions. What a medical student wants from the AMA can be quite different from a physician who has been in practice for 30 years.

But were all physicians the same? All residents? All medical students?

If so, what would account for why one physician would choose to open an email and another physician with the same experience level and age wouldn't? Why would a third physician choose to unsubscribe altogether?

Just like with the Glad-Lock example, it was time to look at things a little differently.

We started our target segmentation by examining how physicians interacted with the content in our daily email newsletter. Using a scrappy, manual approach, we analyzed our email subject lines and the major content components, grouping them into three major buckets:

1. **Advocacy**: Working for legislative and policy changes that benefit patients and physicians.

2. **Practice management**: How to run a more successful, efficient daily practice in the face of many administrative obstacles.

3. **Research**: Scientific advancements in the field of medicine, including newly published research in *JAMA,* the Journal of the American Medical Association.

When we looked at how our audience was interacting with this content, we found three different groups, with about a third of the audience falling into each category. While there was some overlap, the groups were, in fact, distinct. We confirmed this subsequently using more sophisticated modeling.

In other words, we were treating physicians like they were all interested in the same things, when, in fact, they weren't.

As a result, we shifted our strategy and started aligning our email model to this new content-driven target segmentation of advocacy, practice management, and research. This approach wasn't exactly the one-to-one future vision of Pepper and Rogers, but it did allow us to offer a more personalized approach based on content interest. Not surprisingly, this new approach significantly improved how many people opened and interacted with our email, which had a big impact on our membership marketing.

Common sense, right? Providing more relevant and useful information drives engagement. On the flip side, communicating with people about things they are not interested in is like customer repellent. It doesn't take long for these folks to unsubscribe – both literally from your emails and figuratively from your business.

That doesn't mean everyone on my team jumped on board right away with the more personalized approach. When I described this new email strategy, one person popped up and said she believed that communicating differently with different people was unethical. "No," I said. "That's marketing."

***

While different in sophistication, scope, and audiences, the three target segmentation examples have a lot in common. Each of them led to an advancement in the understanding of the target customer and each had an impact on business growth.

To review, here are the key qualities of a great customer segmentation:

- **Based on data, not opinions**: If you hear someone saying, "everyone feels…" or "I think (because I'm in the target audience)…" you should ask, "Where's the data that proves that?" More than likely, that "data" is based on their own opinions and experiences or anecdotes provided by other people. As I learned at P&G, good brand managers never assume they are in the target audience.

- **Predictive**: A great segmentation separates the target audience in meaningful ways from everyone else, predicting who is and who is not in your target audience. The most predictive indicator of future behavior is current behavior. Demographics by themselves are not likely to be predictive. For instance, the fact that you're an avid runner – a behavior – is much more predictive of your desire to buy running shoes than your age. As far as buying a new pair of running shoes goes, you have much more in common with a fellow runner than you do with someone your own age who doesn't run at all.

- **Actionable**: Knowing what your target audience does and how they think and feel provides insight into how to reach them in the real and digital worlds. You can target those behaviors directly across many digital platforms, including social media (more on that shortly).

The great news is that it has become much easier to conduct this kind of 4-D segmentation research. What might have taken a year or more in the past can be accomplished in a period of months – or less – with a combination of qualitative and online quantitative research. For more sophisticated segmentation studies, it's likely you will need the help of an outside research firm. These research firms have the statistical modeling expertise to identify underlying segments that aren't necessarily apparent to the naked eye. There are many research firms who specialize in this specific kind of research.

Whether you use a research firm or not, the same 4-D process still applies to gathering the underlying data. It is critical that as the business and customer experience leader, you play a central role in defining what data is collected. This step allows you to build your hypotheses about underlying behaviors and attitudes into the research.

***

Once you've done the segmentation research and identified your target audience, there's one step left before you've completed this part of the 10-second customer journey playbook: Translating your "target" into "targeting."

Back in the days of my zipper bag target segmentation breakthrough, we were ecstatic to uncover some of the key differentiating behaviors between our target audience and others, like cooking, gardening, and baking. That meant we could shift our ad dollars into media vehicles that over-indexed on these behaviors, like cooking magazines or the reigning shelter brand of the time, *Martha Stewart Living*. These media vehicles theoretically offered more "target-rich" environments to find our customers, like fishing in a better pond, so to speak.

Fishing in someone else's pond, even if it's better, always comes with limitations. You don't exactly know what's in the pond or what kind of bait to use. It's kind of murky and hard to see in there. And in those days, you certainly couldn't tell how effective your bait was in landing a new customer. Thankfully, today's digital targeting tools and platforms provide more powerful ways to find your audience, with much greater visibility.

Here are five ways to translate your 4-D target into "targeting" in today's digital ponds:

1. **Approximation**: Social platforms let you combine behavioral attributes that together help you find high-potential audiences, just like I did in the *Daily Racing Form* example. Just for fun, I like checking the "Why you received this ad" link on various social platforms to see what those attributes are for me. For a recent men's swimsuit ad I saw, these attributes were:

   a. Traveled frequently.
   b. Went on a beach vacation recently.
   c. Visited other men's swimwear sites.

   That's a heck of a good guess. Or, to put it a different way, that's behavioral targeting. And it's certainly a lot better than just sending the ad to every guy of a certain age and income level.

2. **Search**: You are what you search for. And, of course, searching for anything on the web immediately triggers ads for that product or brand (and possibly others) across every digital platform.

   Search is one of the most efficient forms of digital marketing, because you're starting with folks who have demonstrated interest in your product and are therefore likely prospects. Even better, you can easily quantify the cost of acquiring a customer through this channel. Given the predictive power of search, it is no wonder why companies spend hundreds of billions of dollars on search advertising and why Google is one of the biggest companies in the world. There are businesses, like travel, where search is the primary form of marketing, and understanding what "keywords" translate into travel bookings is the Holy Grail for them.

   How do you succeed in targeting with search, especially if you don't have a gigantic search marketing budget? One of the most important tenets of search engine marketing is to answer the questions that your target audience types into Google. That puts you in a much better position to show up as one of the answers (for free).

3. **Looking at similar products**: I'm astounded at how many brands of protein bars there are. How do I know? Because I clicked on one variety to find out more about it, and that opened the targeting floodgates to every one of their competitors.

4. **Re-targeting**: Anyone who lands on your website has given you a strong indication of interest. Assuming they accept the appropriate cookies on your site, you'll be able to follow them across the digital universe with targeted advertising. Do that… while you still can.

5. **Custom audiences**: Have a good email list? Then you can translate that list into a custom audience on social media platforms that reaches only the people on your email list. Many social media platforms will match up users on their site (with appropriate privacy safeguards, and they don't retain the email address) against your list, so you can reach only those users. It's kind of like having your own paid broadcast network. This is a very efficient way of reaching existing customers and identifying prospects for future purchases.

***

Data privacy concerns have fueled increasing international and domestic regulation, already affecting the ability to "fish in someone else's digital pond." The availability of third-party targeting information, often derived through a marketplace of cookies put on a potential target's device through code on a website, will be disappearing. That means having "first-party" information – the kind that you own, with appropriate consent from users – will become even more important to targeting in the future.

It's your job to build that database of first-party knowledge, so you can be in control of and more efficient with your digital fishing. Essentially, you'll use your own digital platform to build an enormous customer list. But how do you do that? How can you know that one website visitor is truly a "qualified" potential customer? By getting these prospective customers to raise their hands and let you know who they are and how to communicate with them.

Here are seven ways to make this happen:

1. **Account creation and login**: Getting someone to create an account that they log into is a phenomenal way to establish customer identity. It's also a great way to reduce

friction in the customer journey by providing the ability to store payment and other information that shortens the checkout process. An account allows your customers to set preferences and raise their hands for information they'd like to receive, such as newsletters. That's why so many sites encourage you to establish an account when you're checking out. Make sure you're communicating the value of account creation. Otherwise, it will be "guest checkout" forever.

2. **Apps**: Apps make frequent purchases a million times easier for customers on mobile devices. But they also generate a treasure trove of usage and purchase information that can be leveraged in personalized communication and loyalty programs (yes, I know it's Double Star Day at Starbucks).

3. **Email address collection**: Again, if you have a customer's email address, you have an audience. This is why companies go to such great lengths to get them. Ever take a quiz about what size pants or shirts will fit you best, or what protein supplement mix is ideal for you, only to find the answer is available only with your email address? Or wonder why you're asked to start an online checkout process with your email? Because an email address, well-used, is digital gold.

4. **Content tagging**: In the AMA segmentation example, we looked at how different audiences interacted with our email newsletters, based on their personal content interests. The same principle applies to content on a website. By properly outfitting your website (called "tagging"), you can begin to identify usage patterns among your site users. This will help you go deeper in your targeting and segmentation approach by getting more granular about user interests beyond general website categories. For instance, if we know that someone is a frequent visitor

to AMA's health equity or well-being content on our site, we can re-target them with other content they're likely to be interested in.

5. **Newsletters**: Great newsletters that provide real value to your customers are a critical way to generate first-party knowledge. With a newsletter, it is easy to tell if you are delivering value by analyzing your open, click-through, and unsubscribe rates. And because newsletters carry unique tracking codes and email addresses, you can learn a lot about customers' online content interests. That's why some sites, like the *New York Times*, provide many different newsletter subscription options and topics tailored to user interests.

6. **Premium content**: "Premium content," the kind you can get access to only with an email address (or subscription), is another classic approach for collecting email addresses and identifying potential customers. Many digital news organizations put certain content behind a gate or paywall for premium subscriptions, like I mentioned with the *Daily Racing Form*. Sometimes this is done with a "hard" gate, where access is available only to subscribers. Other times, companies use a metered approach that gives users a sample, often in exchange for an email address that identifies you as an interested user. If you only access a site for a few articles a month, this exchange can be a reasonable deal for both you and the website.

7. **Browser alerts**: Browser alerts are another form of subscribing users to your site. Instead of asking website users to sign up for a newsletter, you ask the user to subscribe through their web browser. You have probably seen this in action while reading an article on a website. A message pops up asking whether you would like more information on the same topic in the future. If you agree,

then in the future, you will see a browser alert that lets you know a new piece of relevant content is available. While this approach doesn't provide an email address, it is still a high-value subscription for both the content producer and online reader.

***

If you hadn't thought about customer *definition* as the first step in customer experience, then hopefully this chapter changed your mind. At a minimum, you should be able to appreciate the impact of a data-driven customer definition on identifying *and* finding the right audience in the digital world. But once you find your target customer, what are you going to say?

Remember, the clock is ticking. You only have a few seconds. Will you say too much? Too little? Or just the right thing that makes someone feel like a fast friend?

In the next chapter, we'll cover Step 2 of the playbook, which I call "Get The Nod."

Chapter 4
Get The Nod

Creating a compelling brand proposition – or, as some call it, brand *positioning* – has always been a centerpiece of marketing. Successful brands clearly define what they stand for and what benefits they'll deliver to customers in a way that is unique relative to other alternatives in the market.

A great brand proposition is a little like Mr. Spock on *Star Trek*, a combination of logic and human emotion. In the parlance of advertising, the brand proposition melds the "functional benefits" of the product (what it does) with an "emotional insight" into the customer's life (how they feel).

Done well, this combination of function and emotion makes a quick and powerful impression on a prospective customer, eliciting the highly scientific, mental, and physical human reaction known as "The Nod." OK, "scientific" is a stretch. But The Nod is achieved the moment a customer understands what your product does and how it could fit into their lives.

How do you know if you've gotten The Nod? Easy. The Nod gets customers to click in seconds.

This chapter of the playbook will cover some of the key principles of building a digital-ready brand proposition that delivers The Nod. And I'll share a few examples from my past that illustrate how you can put those principles into action.

***

The big difference between a traditional brand proposition and a digital-ready brand proposition comes down to one word: Time. This book is entitled *The 10-Second Customer Journey* for a reason. In the digital world, you just don't get more than a few seconds to catch someone's attention and get them to believe in you. Your brand proposition needs to be so strong, so clear, and so telegraphic that it can withstand the whirlwind tornado funnel.

Here's a quick way to know whether you have a digital-ready brand proposition: You can explain it in one sentence and three bullet points. I call this one-line, three bullet points approach "thinking like a landing page" because it emulates the format of one of the digital world's most valuable pieces of real estate.

A landing page is a standalone web page – typically not a website's homepage – designed to communicate the brand proposition in the simplest and most compelling way possible. The landing page is usually where you'd "land" if you clicked on a digital ad.

The objective of the landing page is to drive the customer to take action, either by buying your product or at least giving you their contact information for follow-up communication. It's incredibly important that the landing page works, or in digital marketing terms, "converts." That's why a landing page is one of the most heavily tested pages in the digital world.

The one-line, three bullet points approach is remarkably similar to the format I learned at P&G more than 30 years ago, long before digital marketing. In those days, I think we used to call it "copy strategy." The first line was the "strategy," and the bullet points were the "support."

Either way, the idea is the same. *Thinking like a landing page* forces discipline. It requires you to find just the right set of words to get The Nod in a few seconds. If you can't boil down your proposition to this format, you've missed the mark and need to start again.

Some companies still miss the memo on this approach. I am amazed that I still see brand propositions that are a paragraph long, full of flowery, non-consumer language. These often focus solely on what the product "is" with an endless list of features. That's a mistake. It's rare that a litany of product features moves the needle. First of all, who has the time to read and absorb the list and translate that into a unique personal benefit? Nobody.

Customers aren't buying a list of features or functionality; they're buying an idea and a solution. And to turn functionality into a solution, you need to combine it with "emotional insight."

Emotional insight demonstrates that you understand how the customer thinks, feels, and lives, and in turn, recognizes how your product will fit into their lives. While this portion of the brand proposition is referred to as the emotional insight, don't take that too literally. The emotional component is not about making customers feel like *crying*. It's about making them feel *understood*.

Let me give you a few examples of ads I've seen recently that had great emotional insight. All of them got me to nod and click through:

- **Protein supplement**: Whey protein makes me feel bloated and there are a lot of calories in two scoops. I started searching for alternatives, and not surprisingly an ad ran through my Instagram feed that said, "Not all protein sources are equal." NOD. I clicked through to their site to learn more about how different kinds of proteins break down into amino acids in the body. I ended up buying their supplement.

- **Dog toy**: Do you become impatient like me when you're walking your dog, and all she wants to do is stop and sniff? I learned from a dog toy ad that sniffing is not only natural for dogs but also healthy. NOD. I clicked to find out more about how their toy engages dogs with active sniffing.

- **Towel**: I love a thick towel but hate how long it takes to dry. Then I learned that "A towel doesn't have to be thick to be absorbent." I was intrigued by this notion. NOD. I clicked through to read more about how their super-thin, larger towels are bigger and dry faster.

Go see for yourself. Next time you're scrolling through your social media feed, which ads get The Nod from you? What is it about the product proposition that intrigued you and got you to click and learn more? How quickly from the moment you saw the ad did you buy something?

Chances are the ads that you responded to combined great product features with emotional insight. Here are four additional qualities that I see in propositions that get The Nod and spark the 10-second customer journey:

1. **Authentic**: Your insight needs to be real, or you will never get a customer to nod. I once came across a proposed insight statement that read, "Consumers are looking for new ways to enjoy the taste of salsa." And the brand proposition? "Here's a new way to enjoy the taste of salsa." I'm guessing no one in the history of chips and salsa has ever said that.

2. **Promise, not product features**: A great brand proposition combines functionality with an emotional insight into the target audience. The combination of those two things forms an idea – a single thing to hold in their mind. Want to send someone packing? Throw a list of features at them.

3. **About the customer**: Remember, a great value proposition is not about what your company or product does. It's about what your company or product does *for the customer.* This benefit-based approach is not second nature to everyone, especially in the nonprofit space, where organizations more frequently recite their mission statement to communicate who they are. In general, mission statements are lofty and inspirational, not customer focused.

4. **Grounded**: There are a lot of "phony" words in marketing, the kind that sound good to marketers but don't mean a lot to the average person. Words like "inspire" and "empower" fall into this category for me. These are words that make marketers feel good but aren't reality for customers. For instance, I recently read an article about how a very popular shoe brand "empowers people's creativity." My eyes could not roll farther into the back of my head.

***

Developing a digital-ready brand proposition is hard work. There's no shortcut to understanding customers. You have to listen and learn through qualitative and quantitative research to make the connections between what your product does and what it can do for your customer. While it's not possible to see a prospective customer's nod as they encounter your digital marketing, you can count the clicks and conversions.

When I talk about the process of getting to a digital-ready brand proposition, I'm sometimes met with blank stares. The art and science of positioning is not second nature outside of the consumer marketing world. To help get the concepts across to people who might not be as familiar, I tell a lot of stories about my past brand positioning experiences. I learned so much from this first example that it changed the course of my career.

But this first case study is important for another reason. Who'd have thought people could have an emotional connection to their plastic containers?

Case study: GladWare plastic containers

While I had worked on a number of consumer brands before I started working at P&G, I'd never created a brand proposition from scratch. Then came GladWare plastic containers.

I now work across the Chicago River from the Leo Burnett office where it all started, more than 25 years ago. I remember vividly being in my office one Saturday afternoon writing concept statements for upcoming focus group research. We were testing a new product idea – a reusable plastic container that was far less expensive than premium alternatives like Rubbermaid and Tupperware but better than what you'd get for free at the deli counter.

Initial customer feedback on the idea of a higher quality, reusable plastic container was middling. Yes, the focus group participants appreciated that the containers worked well. Had a tight lid. Went into the dishwasher. Were stackable. But they were not compelled. There was something missing, but prior to that day, I couldn't figure out what that something was. What was missing?

Insight.

As I thought through what we had heard in our focus group research, it struck me: Our audience had an emotional attachment to their plastic containers. Yes, even a relationship with a plastic container could be emotional. For starters, plastic storage containers cost a lot, so if you lent one to a friend and she didn't return it, you held a sometimes friendship-altering grudge. If you packed it in your spouse's lunch and it got lost or ruined in the microwave, you were annoyed. The folks we talked to were so upset about losing or ruining a container that they often refused to throw away any containers they'd accumulated, whether they had a matching lid or not. As surprising as it was, one thing was crystal clear: We hadn't thought about the emotional connection to something as seemingly unemotional as a plastic container.

Then I wrote down this line: *The containers you'll love to use and can afford to lose.*

This one sentence spoke directly to the anxiety that the research showed our audience was feeling about their plastic containers. It touched a nerve. This product was more than a container. It was a solution to plastic container anxiety.

That concept language inspired our one-line, three-bullet, digital-ready brand proposition for GladWare plastic containers, which read:

A plastic container you don't have to worry about.

- *Closes securely*
- *Dishwasher safe*
- *Costs about $1 per container*

In other words, it did the job, could be reused, and didn't alter your friendships or marriage if it got lost or damaged.

The TV commercials featured humorous takes on plastic container anxiety, with one featuring a woman asking her husband to swear an oath to protect the container. The tagline, "The container you'll love to use and can afford to lose," went from my concept page into the commercials and onto the package for many years.

That was the beginning of an entirely new grocery category and a multi-million-dollar business.

I think of this approach to developing a brand proposition as the "Leo Burnett Way," and it has stuck with me as I've moved from brand to brand and from the physical world into the digital world. This approach combines both the functional aspects of the product (what it does) with an emotional insight that gets The

Nod. Adding insight to function made customers feel understood and recognized.

I carried this approach into my work in digital product management and website general management. That doesn't mean being an evangelist of this philosophy has been easy. Unlike in the consumer marketing world, this approach was unfamiliar to a lot of digital businesses people I encountered and was often met with skepticism.

Case study: Major League Gaming

This next example comes from a world far from plastic containers – video games.

When you hear the term "gamers," you might think of pimply-faced teenagers spending hours in a dark basement glued to a screen playing a game like Call of Duty. That would be an inaccurate generalization. Gaming is pretty universal, and there are now professional gamers who make hundreds of thousands of dollars while spending their days competing in online games of all types, from Madden Football to Fortnight.

In one of the gaming chapters of my career, I was the General Manager of Digital for a startup called Major League Gaming, one of the first professional video gaming leagues. We held live tournaments across the country where teams would compete for a $1 million-dollar prize, which was unheard of at the time. The top players were superstars with big followings.

But as we started to think about growing the business, we realized we needed to move beyond the small population of elite professionals battling it out for millions of dollars in prize money and superstar status. So, we started with, yes, you guessed it, a new look at the target audience using the 4-D segmentation approach discussed in the last chapter.

Using the 4-D approach, we identified a large segment of "aspiring amateurs" who wanted to learn from the elite professional players. These gamers probably would never end up playing for millions of dollars at a live tournament. But they were interested in honing their skills in online tournaments, watching videos about professional players, reading articles about gaming strategy, and following guidance from the "pros" about the latest games.

As part of the research, our agency, McKinney, had already conducted video interviews with aspiring amateurs who came to watch the pro teams play at one of our events. I'll never forget the video montage the agency put together that revealed the "emotional connection" we needed to complete our proposition. Imagine a series of 30 gamers asked to choose a single word to describe themselves, then all responding with the same answer:

> *"I'm competitive. I'm competitive. I'm competitive. I'm competitive."*
> *Over and over. (Light bulb turns on.)*

While these aspiring amateurs would never be pro players, their level of competitiveness was a defining behavioral and attitudinal characteristic.

We used this knowledge to create and test proposition statements in our quantitative 4-D research. When we analyzed our results, we found a winning statement that got The Nod:

> *Know where you stand and how to get better.*

This statement helped us knit together the functional aspects of the business, including an online tournament platform, our live events, and digital content into a meaningful proposition for a wider enthusiast audience.

Remember in the previous chapter how talking to the "right" audience can inspire new product ideas? Well, as a North Star for our programming and product work, the new customer definition and proposition statement opened our eyes to a big new opportunity.

A new version of the top video game Halo included a feature that made it possible for players to capture and upload their game play for the first time. To me, watching video game footage is not anywhere as good as watching *Squid Game*, but this was an enthusiast audience that simply couldn't get enough. So, we decided to celebrate the Halo launch with a contest to see who could capture the coolest footage from the new game.

Not everyone on the team was thrilled with the amount of energy we were putting into this contest, but a few days later, I noticed our website traffic taking off like a rocket. I thought it had to be a mistake. As we passed by one million unique users – three times our normal traffic – it became apparent what was happening. One of our contestants had submitted the most insane footage of a ricocheting kill shot, and it became a viral hit that sent our traffic into the stratosphere, never to return to prior levels.

Despite the demonstrated potential of the new positioning, I faced a lot of resistance from others in the company, many of them gamers themselves. One person told me he didn't believe in the strategy of having professional gamers dispensing advice, saying that it was beneath them. A professional basketball player, in this person's mind, would never do that.

This attitude was relatively pervasive, and the organization remained focused primarily on the pro-level players and live event model. Unfortunately, not following the new proposition to its fullest potential closed off a big opportunity. Just how big?

Billions.

Just a year later, a company called Twitch launched a video channel devoted solely to game play. Twitch, eventually purchased by Amazon, generated nearly $3 billion in revenue in 2022[1] and is worth about $45 billion.[2]

In retrospect, I wonder what would have happened if we had embraced the learning about our customer and digital brand proposition and centered our strategy around video game play instead of live-tournament play. Hindsight is 20/20, but that's one of the lessons I've learned. It is easy to get locked into your product model and lose sight of the opportunities a redefined target and brand proposition can bring to light. I wish I'd been visionary enough to see that.

***

So far, we've talked about developing digital-ready brand propositions for two very different audiences: Plastic container users and video gamers. Hopefully, you're getting the point that no matter how varied the audience, the same approach will help you identify a compelling proposition that gets The Nod. In fact, I applied these same principles to horseplayers and then to an entirely different audience in my current CXO role: Physicians.

This next case study demonstrates not only the power of a compelling brand proposition, but also how a great proposition stands the test of time, whatever the circumstances. In fact, once you establish a brand proposition, it turns out to be remarkably difficult to get customers to think about you in a different way. That's why it's so important to get it right because *repositioning* is very time consuming and expensive. What you can change is your

---

[1] Available from: www.businessofapps.com/data/twitch-statistics/ [Accessed 13 February 2024].
[2] Available from: https://markets.businessinsider.com/news/stocks/ twitch-s-dominant-market-position-could-turn-into-high-margin-growth-driver-for-amazon-says-analyst-1032228327 [Accessed 13 February 2024].

marketing campaign, which brings the brand proposition to life in ads and other media.

Case study: American Medical Association

A lot of people were perplexed about my move from horse racing to the world of medicine. While the context was very different, there were some interesting similarities. First, both the *Daily Racing Form* and the AMA were older organizations, having been around for more than 125 years and 175 years, respectively. Second, the audience size was about the same. There are 1.5 million horseplayers and 1.5 million physicians, resident physicians, and medical students. Third, as far as digital media goes, both horseplayers and physicians fall into the category of "enthusiast audiences" who can't get enough of their respective content categories. Finally, under the hood, running a digital data subscription operation closely tied to horse racing content turns out to be remarkably similar to running a membership operation tied closely to health care content.

For an organization as old, well-established, and recognizable in the United States as the AMA, I was surprised at how little many prospective and current members knew about what the organization was doing.

It did not take a brain surgeon to diagnose why I was constantly met with the refrain, "I don't know what the AMA does." The work on behalf of physicians and patients was excellent. But the marketing of the work and its value to members needed to be dialed up. First, there was clearly an issue with how we were articulating the brand proposition. If you asked what the AMA did, you would typically hear a recitation of the AMA's mission statement or a list of initiatives we were working on. While these answers were technically accurate, they didn't constitute the kind of digital-ready brand proposition we've discussed. We needed to build a proposition that combined both "function" and "emotion" if we wanted to drive membership growth.

I used the same approach we have talked about in the previous case studies; a combination of qualitative and quantitative 4-D research to understand our customers. For starters, here's one thing you learn very fast about physicians: They have a calling to practice medicine and help patients. Me? When my wife has a tiny cold, I shift into full germaphobe mode. But physicians? They run toward this kind of thing.

In order to practice medicine, physicians go through the wringer – more than a decade of post-college education and training, including a grueling residency, and often more than $200,000 in student-loan debt.[3] Once they are finally able to start practicing medicine, they face myriad obstacles in doing what they love to do, from handling a massive amount of paperwork, wrangling with insurance companies, struggling with reimbursement rates, and sometimes dealing with political interference.

Being a doctor is a tough enough job already. Physicians needed someone in their corner to clear the obstacles between them and patient care. Someone with the power to make a difference that an individual on their own can't. This insight provided the emotional connection we needed to add to "the work" to create our digital-ready brand proposition:

Physicians' Powerful Ally in Patient Care™

- *Speaking with a unified voice*
- *Removing obstacles to patient care*
- *Fighting public health crises*
- *Driving the future of medicine*

---

[3] Available from: https://educationdata.org/average-medical-school-debt [Accessed 20 February 2024].

Yes, I did cheat and add a fourth bullet point, but it was necessary to capture what the brand delivered. Research confirmed the power of our brand proposition and showed that just reading the one line and four bullet points made the problem of "I don't know what you do" go away.

From *Physicians' Powerful Ally in Patient Care* (the brand proposition) came "Members Move Medicine" (the marketing campaign). The campaign told the story of what the AMA was delivering to physicians and students through the voices of our members. The bullet points of the brand proposition provided a framework for us to deliver the "proof" and value of our initiatives.

The campaign worked, driving growth in membership and increases in awareness of our initiatives and brand strength. Our members loved seeing themselves – instead of stock photos – featured in all our advertising and promotional materials.

Had nothing else changed, we probably could have continued the "Members Move Medicine" campaign for a long time. But something unexpected happened that required us to re-evaluate the campaign approach.

In 2020, the COVID-19 pandemic hit. What it meant to be *Physicians' Powerful Ally in Patient Care* took on a different meaning in that moment.

Now, notice I said we needed to re-evaluate our *campaign*, not our *brand proposition*. A sign of a great brand proposition is that it endures, despite the circumstances. In fact, at that moment, physicians needed a powerful ally more than ever.

Working as a team, we carefully adapted our three bullet points of support to address an entirely different environment:

- Being a definitive and trusted resource of information on the prevention, diagnosis, and treatment of COVID-19, in the face of a torrent of misinformation.

- Working at the highest levels to remove obstacles to patient care – literally helping keep offices open and physicians safe.

- Amplifying the voices and needs of physicians and channeling them into action.

Every part of our organization shifted its activities to focus on how to deliver to physicians and patients in this environment, from governmental advocacy to helping physician offices stay open, securing and distributing protective equipment, and helping launch telemedicine services. We even launched a new daily video where our leaders could keep physicians up to date.

Due to the COVID-19 pandemic, we paused our membership solicitation (as in, the "ask" to join) for a good portion of 2020. But we increased our communications to ensure physicians were aware of our efforts and our initiatives to support them. Rather than facing a significant decline in membership, we grew substantially. Why? Because we focused on customer experience, working together to deliver for our audience.

And our audience responded.

When the acute phase of the pandemic was behind us, our research pointed to another shift in the needs of our audience. While the pandemic had subsided, all the problems in health care that existed before the pandemic were magnified – physician burnout, administrative burdens like prior authorization, reimbursement issues, health disparities… you name it. Physicians clearly were asking for more support as we transitioned into this uncertain new world.

I found myself feeling very frustrated at the predicament physicians were in. Here was a group of people who literally put their lives on the line to get our nation through the pandemic, but now it seemed as though the nation was forgetting their sacrifices and not accounting for the devastating blow this had dealt the profession. So, one night, when I was thinking about what to do, I scratched down a few lines that captured how I was feeling:

For two long years, you took care of this nation. Now it's time this nation takes care of you. We need a recovery plan for America's physicians.

Again, there was no change in our brand proposition. It was still all about being *Physicians' Powerful Ally in Patient Care*. But what it meant in that moment and how it was supported had to adapt to the needs of our audience. The idea of a "recovery plan for America's physicians" resonated with our members. Why? Because it grew out of insight and "packaged" five important streams of work into a single idea:

1. Addressing physician well-being and burnout – the highest rates on record.

2. Reforming the Medicare payment system.

3. Reducing administrative burdens like prior authorization.

4. Ensuring physician leadership of the health care team.

5. Supporting telemedicine, which became incredibly important in the pandemic.

These five areas reflected the top concerns of our audience, and they became our laser focus.

The recovery plan has proven to be a powerful and compelling marketing campaign. As an expression of our brand positioning, the recovery plan is a great example of how you can adapt your marketing campaign and messages without changing your core, enduring brand proposition.

***

The three "proposition" case studies in this chapter were very different – plastic containers, live video gaming events, and a medical association. But the approach to developing the proposition was the same. Additionally, each case study demonstrates how a brand proposition helps shape the nature of the product. That's why the brand proposition is such an important step in my CXO playbook.

In the next chapter, you'll see just how important positioning is to creating great products. And I'll share some of the CXO secrets I've learned along the way about product development and avoiding the pitfalls that lead to "products that suck."

Chapter 5
Creating products that don't suck

If you skipped ahead because you thought the chapter on product development is where all the action would be, well, I can't say I blame you. Product development is exciting. Unlike the first two steps of my playbook – defining your target audience and developing your brand proposition – "product" is tangible. Who doesn't want to see their brilliant idea brought to life and generate millions of dollars?

I'm not Steve Jobs, but I have had a few good bites at the product apple (pun intended) in my lifetime. I know what product success tastes like, and it is delicious. Fortunately, I discovered early in my career that the real fun is translating insight about the target customer into a compelling brand proposition, then developing a product that delivers. That's why working on GladWare plastic containers was such a pivotal learning experience for me. Following the right process created a template that I've been using for decades since.

Here's what's not fun: Working on a product that sucks.

Oh, yes. I've worked on a product that sucked. Actually, I've worked on multiple products that sucked. For example:

- An aspirin product designed to be easier on the stomach but took longer to relieve pain. Fail.

- An antiperspirant for guys with super-thick underarm hair, which unfortunately turned your shirts yellow. Fail.

- A PC-based app that lets you "green screen" yourself into famous movie scenes. Sounded fun, until you actually tried to do it. (One of the most embarrassing moments of my life was doing a demo of the product on live TV where I accidentally hit the wrong button on my laptop.) Fail.

Eric Ries, author of the brilliant book *The Lean Startup*, has a perfect term to describe the process of creating products that suck. He calls it "achieving failure," or "successfully building a product that no one wants." While the concepts in *The Lean Startup* were geared originally to smaller, fast-growing tech companies, the principles apply to pretty much every organization. I especially love his term "product-market fit" which describes alignment between two of the Xs in customer experience. Sometimes, I wish Ries had called it "market-product fit" to emphasize the importance of understanding the customer first before iterating on the product itself.

Ries also recommended that marketing should play an important role in product development from the get-go. His viewpoint is an important recognition that successful product development is a team sport. And as a customer experience team leader, the CXO plays an important role in developing products that customers actually want. This chapter focuses on four ways I've learned that a CXO can add value to the product development process and pave the way for a successful 10-second customer journey:

- Building marketing into product development.

- Stopping bad product initiatives.

- Ensuring alignment between the Xs.

- Packaging product offerings for the customer.

Building marketing into product development

I am a strong advocate of placing a sign in every product development operation reminding folks not to start product initiatives without completing the prior two steps of this playbook: Defining the target audience and developing a digital-ready brand (or product) proposition. Consider this your sign.

Job #1 is to ensure that the first two playbook steps are done and done well. I've learned from experience not to take it for granted that these steps have been completed, even with a product that has been in-market for a while and "doing fine." For starters, a fresh pair of eyes and a new approach to customer definition might yield insights that lead to better marketing and accelerated growth. The zipper bag case study we discussed earlier in the book is a perfect example. Taking a closer look at the brand or product proposition is essential as well, especially in situations where growth has slowed. Markets and customers are not stagnant. There may be a new competitor with a stronger offering, or perhaps an underlying change in customer needs. For instance, at the AMA, we built an online education platform that helps residency institutions meet critical educational requirements established a decade ago. Since then, some institutions have taken their own approach to meeting those requirements. So, to continue to grow the reach of our platform, we had to evolve our proposition beyond merely "meeting requirements."

It is critical to bring marketing into the mix for customer definition and brand proposition work because most product development teams aren't structured or skilled in this area. Of course, at this stage, research and product testing are essential to ensure that the product delivers on the proposition and to identify any significant issues. Beyond product testing, there are two additional important reasons why the marketing/product collaboration is so important at this stage.

First, it takes time to build a great marketing plan. Yet so many times, there is a near-cliché dynamic of "here's the product, go market it." This last-minute pivot to marketing is common because it's easy to spend all your time working on the product and leave the thinking about marketing for the end. Thus, if you find yourself in a product meeting early in the process and the team is spending 90% of its time talking about the product and 10% or less on marketing, raise a red flag. That split should be at least 50/50. Why? Even good product ideas without detailed, sound, long-term marketing plans will, at best, succeed less than they should. At worst, poor marketing planning can lead to failure.

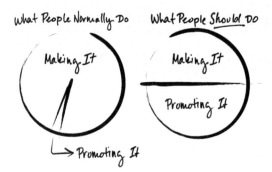

Second, in the world of digital products, it is essential to build marketing *into* the product. This typically involves a combination of both analytic tools and "upselling." I've seen many a website or new application launched without being properly outfitted with analytics, making it impossible to measure progress, analyze the marketing funnel, or identify friction points. Trying to add appropriate analytics after the fact can take a lot of time that you don't have during a product launch, when there is a lot of pressure and you're fielding a ton of questions. These analytic elements also aid in the process of upselling, or getting customers to spend more through premium features, add-ons, merchandising, and loyalty programs. Upsells are a critical revenue engine for any shopping or gaming site. Who can resist upsells like "customers also bought" or "spend $10 more and get free shipping"?

A marketing/product collaboration early in the process is essential to identifying the appropriate metrics, analytics, and upsell opportunities and having them built in, not retrofitted.

Stopping bad product initiatives

Here's one thing I have observed throughout my career: Once people start working on a new product initiative, it is extremely tough to stop the momentum. It takes someone with the right level of organizational authority to shut down a product initiative, even if everyone knows it's unlikely to succeed.

Wait, isn't stopping product initiatives the opposite of growth? Not at all. It's a matter of focus. Typically, there are often more product initiatives under way than resources to support them. Less promising projects sap energy and resources from more promising ones.

For example, when I arrived at the AMA, the team had just developed a detailed journey map outlining every step of the journey from medical student to physician. Certain decisions or inflection points along the way corresponded to potential new product ideas. For example, the journey map identified fears about student debt as a common issue for medical students. As a result, work started on a digital app to help medical students assess and deal with student debt.

That's not to say that such an app couldn't be useful. But it also would have been costly and time consuming to develop and market. As the CXO, I looked at that initiative and asked, "Wouldn't it be better to just write articles about navigating student debt instead?" After all, we already had a top-notch content team and access to financial experts and physicians who had gone through the process successfully. On top of that, AMA members were accustomed to finding "news you can use" on our existing channels, so we did not face the obstacle of promoting adoption of an entirely new product. Writing an article and marketing it in the appropriate places was considerably less expensive and much easier to disseminate to medical students than inventing a new student debt management tool.

Ensuring alignment between the Xs

We've already talked about the importance of up-front collaboration between marketing and product. But for a product initiative to be successful, there needs to be complete alignment across all four Xs of experience, including commerce (the revenue model) and service. I learned this the hard way.

At the turn of the millennium, I was a director of product management at AOL's city guide startup, Digital City. I oversaw a portfolio of commerce-driven products, including online personal ads (the original digital dating app) and the Yellow Pages online business directory. When I saw the success that another company was having by tying user reviews to products, I had an idea: What if we could leverage the personal profiles engine with the Yellow Pages business database to enable people to start reviewing local businesses?

Sound vaguely familiar?

I convinced my boss to let me sequester myself and a developer away to build this. A few months later, we created the "Digital

City Local Experts" application. It was easy to use. Just build a quick profile, find a local business, and write a review.

Right out of the gate, users began to create tens of thousands of reviews on everything from dry cleaners to auto dealers. I was ecstatic.

Then, reality hit. Some of those auto dealers and other businesses were our advertisers, and when they read their own bad reviews, they howled. I would then get a call from our salespeople and account managers, imploring me to take down the review.

This was clearly not going to be a very scalable national platform. In fact, the more the "product" succeeded, the more problems it created. Ultimately, our city guide startup was absorbed fully into AOL, and we were all reorganized. Without a champion, the Local Experts product was neglected and eventually died a quiet, digital death.

This experience makes me sad for a couple reasons.

First, in hindsight, Local Experts could have been a giant idea if there had been full X-alignment from the start. The user-generated review approach theoretically could have been "the product" around which local advertisers bought templatized, possibly self-service ads. Instead, we were producing more expensive digital products like news and entertainment guides. This content was the product around which sales teams sold to local advertisers in major cities across the United States. Only one of these models was scalable (hint, not the one we were executing).

Granted, AOL Local Experts was also ahead of its time. Remember, this was around the year 2000. This was well before the mainstreaming of search ads and, of course, mobile, which paved the way for the ultimate winners in this paradigm: Yelp and Google.

But technology aside, I couldn't see at the time just how naïve I'd been to miss the X factor that is at the heart of this book

– product-marketing-commerce-service alignment. We had what proved to be an appealing product. The market was there, as demonstrated by the deluge of reviews that poured in soon after we flipped the switch. But the commerce and service parts? They were out of alignment. Without that full four-pillar X-experience alignment, this initiative was destined to fail.

Packaging product offerings for the customer

Sometimes, it's not what's *in* the product that sells. It's what's *around* it. The term for this is "packaging," and it means different things in traditional consumer products than it does in the digital world.

Traditionally, packaging meant the physical container that held your product. Physical packaging is and remains extremely important. Apple made packaging into an art form. There is an entire video genre called "unboxing" which pays homage to packaging. Shocker: Nearly 80% of wine sales are based on the label alone.[1]

But for digital companies, packaging isn't about the physical container. It's about how digital "things" (or "assets" as we call them) are put together and presented to the customer. From a customer's point of view, the premise of packaging is simple: It is easier for someone to hold *one* idea in their mind than it is to remember a bunch of stuff.

One of the most basic approaches of packaging is "bundling." This kind of packaging was the mainstay of the cable industry until consumers began cord cutting. If you ever looked at hooking up cable or internet service at a home or an apartment in the past

---

[1] Available from: www.winebusiness.com/news/article/177492 [Accessed 13 February 2024].

few decades, you will likely have been bombarded with "Triple Play" offers that bundle what you want in TV with internet and phone service. The more services cable companies could hook you up with, the more revenue they could generate. Often, bundle packages have "multi-product" discounts that provide a disincentive for dropping one of the services. It was a great approach while it lasted. (I'm sorry, what's a home phone?)

In the digital and the media worlds, packaging goes beyond bundling alone to provide a more attractive customer or advertiser solution. For example, media companies – whether they be TV networks or traditional print publishers – might have a difficult time selling mass quantities of standard television spots or print ad spaces by themselves. But packaged together with ownership of a halftime show or most valuable player award, these units not only fly out the door faster, but they also come with the premium of an added value sponsorship layer. In other words, you're not just selling a product, you're selling the experience of owning something bigger and more exclusive.

Ideally, the packaging of these individual ad and media-based components can form a "solution" to a customer problem. As an example, I recently saw a social media post from my old company, the *Daily Racing Form*, about a "Raceboost" package. This is a package I came up with when I worked there years ago. We marketing types love it when an idea we helped create outlives our tenure at the business! In this case, I was gratified to see that more than a decade after I made up the term "Raceboost," it was still in use and driving revenue.

Raceboost is a digital package targeted at advertisers, specifically horse racing tracks, that is a classic combination of the Xs – product, marketing, commerce, and service. The package was positioned as a surefire way for racetracks to boost betting on important race days. Instead of just standard ads, the package included additional print and digital editorial content, a video race preview, and high-level promotion on the website homepage and in the important "Entries" section. The entries offering was especially important, since this is the first stop horseplayers go to see what horses are running in each race. As an added element, we included special deals on the data packages that players use for betting. The combination of all these components was not an accident or a dart thrown at some marketing dartboard. It derived from countless conversations with our racetrack clients and salespeople. More importantly than that, it was a win–win relative to what our target horseplayer audience was looking for as well.

With that success, I learned to apply the same digital packaging principles we used for racetrack advertisers to an entirely different advertising customer: Breeding farms.

Where do successful stallions go after winning high-profile horse races? They go to breeding farms, many of which are located in Kentucky. Google "Todd Unger NYT American Pharaoh" and you'll find a picture of me with the majestic Triple Crown winner, who now "stands" at Coolmore Farm in Lexington, Kentucky. Breeding farms like Coolmore are a critically important part of the horse racing industry, as they literally help create winning horses. These farms are high-stakes operations. A top breeding stallion earns tens of thousands – even hundreds of thousands – of dollars each time they breed.

From an advertising standpoint, racetrack and breeding farm customers are very different. Racetracks are focused on promoting *what is to come*. Breeders are most interested in promoting *what happened*. When a horse wins a race, breeders specifically want potential customers to know who the father (sire) is. Should it be one of their stallions, a win from a sire's offspring equals money for the breeder.

Creating an appealing breeder package meant product innovation:

- We changed our popular "Results" section to incorporate the names of the sires.

- We called the new product "Sire-Powered Results."

- Combined with other components of editorial content, ad units, and breeding-based analysis, this new package provided a customer-centric pathway into an entirely new ad category.

We also took these same digital packaging principles and began to apply them to our customers: The horseplayers themselves. I'll never forget my first spring at the *Daily Racing Form*. The first of the three Triple Crown events, the Kentucky Derby, was fast approaching. The Triple Crown races are the three biggest horse races of the year, attracting serious bettors and more casual wagerers alike. It was a big business when I started at the *Daily Racing Form* in 2010, and even bigger now. In 2023, total wagering on the Kentucky Derby Week races broke $400 million for the first time, reaching $412 million from all sources, according to the host track, Churchill Downs. More than $47 million was wagered on the Kentucky Derby alone.

As the "first Saturday in May" (the traditional date of the Derby) approached, I asked my team what we were selling to attract more horseplayers and found out there was really nothing special in the mix.

So, I decided to experiment with the creation of a Kentucky Derby Package. This package bundled unique editorial content, expert handicapper picks for the day, and full-day data access. Yes, we had to produce some additional editorial content, but the other two pieces – the picks and the data – were readily available on the site. Yet packaged together with the editorial content, they created a compelling proposition that was highly merchandisable in a way that selling the three items individually was not.

The Kentucky Derby Package was extremely successful at driving incremental revenue. We decided to replicate the model for the remaining two Triple Crown races, the Preakness and the Belmont

Stakes. From that success story, a greater success story was born. The following year, we started this effort much earlier. We not only sold a package for each individual Triple Crown race, but also began to package all three events together as well. The Triple Crown became what the holiday season is to retailers, with the festivities kicking off earlier and earlier in the year – just without the way-too-early Pumpkin Spice Lattes.

***

I'll never forget the first time I ever heard the term "product development."

In my younger days, I was a bit of a clothes horse (yes, a theme) and was very interested in finding a job in the world of fashion. As part of my search, I networked my way through to a woman who worked at Salvatore Ferragamo in New York City. She mentioned to me that part of her responsibilities included product development. Up until that point, I guess in my somewhat limited world view I pictured this as solely the purview of designers, not businesspeople. It hit me like a lightning bolt. I didn't just want to be in marketing, I wanted to be in product development.

Well, instead of fashion, it ended up being a plastic container. But the feeling was still the same, just somewhat less stylish. With GladWare, I learned a lot about putting the foundation in place for a successful product. Based on our customer knowledge, we had a really great story to tell. In those days, the options for telling that story to the world were pretty limited, but we made the most of it.

I decided to follow my product development dream, but not in the world of consumer products. Instead, I took a leap into my first product management role, at a new and possibly struggling company called America Online. My boss's boss at Leo Burnett told me it was the worst career decision I would ever make. In his mind, this internet thing was just another fad.

But I was about to embark on an entirely new part of my CXO-in-the-making journey and begin my rapid introduction to modern-day storytelling and digital marketing platforms. Suddenly, there were a lot more storytelling options. I had to learn how to use them together to drive growth.

Chapter 6
Telling your story

One of the most famous lines in motion picture history is often misquoted.

In the 1989 classic *Field of Dreams*, star Kevin Costner is walking through an Iowa cornfield when he hears a voice whisper, "If you build it, he will come." Costner goes on to build a baseball field amid the corn, and his creation attracts the ghosts of legendary baseball players. I'm guessing that's why most people think the quote was "If you build it, *they* will come."

Why do I bring up a 30-plus-year-old sports movie? Because many people think that once you have a product that meets an actual need, customers will come flocking to give you their money. But just like the misquote above, that's simply not right. In the world of digital marketing, the inaccurate adage is, well, inaccurate. You can't just create something and think your work is done. You have to find a way to share your product with your target audience. You have to explain to them why your product will make a difference in their lives and solve a pain point of theirs.

The best way to do that is through storytelling.

When it comes to customer experience, stories help people understand a product offering. Building a robust storytelling platform is the key to bringing your product to your customer. And here's the good news: Our attraction to well-told stories is part of our human hardwiring. It turns out that, neurologically, we love stories, so much so that if we encounter something that doesn't have a beginning, middle, and end, our brains will actually create the missing pieces for us to help us make sense of what we're seeing.

In this chapter, we're going to talk about the keys to successful storytelling and how to build such a strong storytelling platform that it can be applied to each and every new product you come up with.

***

Before we get too far into this chapter, let us go over a few keywords that can get people confused: Advertising, storytelling, content marketing, and direct response marketing.

Advertising has always been about telling a brand's story through different media. Going back to the 1950s, there were lots of ways to tell the story, through radio, television, print, and out-of-home advertising like billboards and bus-stop bench advertising.

But when some people these days wax on about the word "storytelling," they mean a more literal approach where you tell a story with a narrative arc, as opposed to what might be considered "selling." In this view, storytelling is a long, soft, indirect approach meant to evoke feelings and spur action, compared with a more direct approach like what you might associate with an infomercial pitch or a plain old ad.

Then there are "content marketing" and "direct response marketing." Content marketing is a form of storytelling that uses content and narrative to slowly build toward a sale. Direct response marketing is geared toward driving an immediate sale.

While there are differences in how these terms are understood, the reality is that the differences are no longer relevant. Why? Because in the world of the 10-second customer journey, whether you are creating a commercial, posting on a social platform, or sending out direct mail, you are always selling.

***

In the pre-tornado funnel days, businesses reached their customers through mass advertising. You bought 30-second TV commercials to tell your story or forked over $40,000 for a page in a top magazine, hoping someone would see and read it. There was neither a "click" that allowed a potential customer to quickly find out more information, nor the ability to close the deal on the spot. Given these limitations, you hoped that at some point you would drive the audience to a store or showroom to pick up your product. Those were the days of retailer John Wanamaker's famous quote, "I know half my advertising is wasted; I just don't know which half."

There will continue to be a TV advertising market for big brands who need mass scale and have the capacity to spend upwards of a million dollars on a 30-second commercial. But if you think back to how this chapter started – talking about the wiring of our brains – you can see why this approach doesn't necessarily suffice. It's one thing to say that the brain is hardwired for stories. That's true. But *your* brain is likely hardwired for a different type of story than mine is. I might like mysteries. You might like a good romance. Someone else hates fiction altogether and reads only biographies. The stories all might have the same basic structure – beginning, middle, and end – but the tale each is telling is far different.

Digital advertising hacked into this mass advertising market and forever changed it. It allowed you to tell the right kind of story to appeal to your target audience without having to spend money on people interested in a different genre. The ability to tell your brand story to only those people who like that kind of story – your target audience – is the reason the TV advertising spending in the United States is expected to fall another 10% over the next five years.[1] That drop is on top of a nearly 8% decline from when spending reached its zenith of $72.4 billion in 2018. That number is expected to drop to $56.83 billion by 2027.[2]

Print media, which once accounted for more than 60% of all global ad spending, has fared far worse – for the very same reason. Putting an ad in the daily paper, which was read by a huge variety of target audiences, meant you were spending money to tell a mystery to a lover of in-depth World War II history. According to a report from intelligence provider WARC, global advertising revenue for total print is projected to total $47.2 billion in 2023, a 7.7% drop from 2022.[3] This continues a trend in which the global ad marketplace for print has fallen by half over the past six years.[4]

***

Digital marketing is a different story. It has been both fascinating and mind-blowing to have lived through and participated in the development of digital marketing over the past 20 years. In that short amount of time, we have seen the birth and expansion of today's digital storytelling platform, a suite of digital tools, social platforms, and products that you can use to reach your

---

[1] Available from: www.statista.com/statistics/272404/tv-advertising-spending-in-the-us/ [Accessed 13 February 2024].

[2] Available from: www.statista.com/statistics/272404/tv-advertising-spending-in-the-us/ [Accessed 13 February 2024].

[3] Available from: www.forbes.com/sites/bradadgate/2023/03/07/global-ad-revenue-for-print-struggles-as-total-ad-revenue-nears-1-trillion/?sh=200d4ad5275a [Accessed 13 February 2024].

[4] Available from: www.forbes.com/sites/bradadgate/2023/03/07/global-ad-revenue-for-print-struggles-as-total-ad-revenue-nears-1-trillion/?sh=200d4ad5275a [Accessed 13 February 2024].

specific customer. Every technological advance has created new opportunities and capabilities for storytelling.

Succeeding in this era has required constant adaptation to changing customer needs and opportunities. This may not be a perfect timetable, but for starters I thought it would be helpful to take a look at how the digital storytelling platform has developed. The following six phases happened in rapid succession and transformed everything about digital marketing and customer experience:

1. **The beginning of internet advertising (mid- to late 90s)**: This kicked off a revolution. Old media models started to show their cracks and we began the transition to the "new media" space. I remember distinctly the huge book cataloging all the places you could stick your online banner ads on the America Online site. This digital real estate was considered so valuable that upstart brands would pay $90 million to be an "anchor tenant" on a popular piece of digital content.

2. **The onset of search advertising (early 2000s)**: With the explosion of internet content and websites, people needed a way to find it all. Enter search engines and the advent of search engine advertising and marketing. Search advertising is probably the single most powerful revolution in digital marketing (thus far). It provides exactly what marketers are always looking for: High-intent potential customers and measurable ROI. Suddenly, marketing leaders could prove they were generating revenue, with data to back it up.

3. **The development of digital advertising exchanges (mid 2000s)**: Up to this point, if you wanted to run your online ad on a particular website, you had to buy ad inventory from that specific site. Since there were literally thousands of websites to choose from, this was not very

efficient for either buyers or sellers, especially for smaller websites. And there was no guarantee that every user on a particular website was in your target audience. But the change ushered in by ad networks was more profound than mere efficiency. It gave advertisers the ability to turn "target" into digital "targeting." Leveraging cookies that tracked users across sites (in that era, without the user's knowledge or consent), ad networks allowed marketers to target specific behavioral profiles, no matter what site the user was on.

4. **The rise of mobile marketing (mid- to late 2000s):** As the number of mobile devices skyrocketed and mobile download speeds increased, website usage shifted rapidly from desktop to mobile viewing. This shift drove major redesigns of websites and ad models to provide users with a "mobile web" experience.

5. **Attack of the apps (late 2000s):** The 2008 launch of Apple's App Store ushered in a whole new world of digital products, marketing, and commerce. Apps provided a much better experience for mobile device users. But apps also gave companies a massive amount of information about in-app behavior that they could leverage to drive additional purchases and revenue.

6. **The power of algorithmic social media advertising (2010s):** Say what you want about the impact of social networks like Facebook, but their sophisticated, algorithm-based delivery of ads and content offered next-level targeting capabilities based on user preferences, activities, and friend networks.

Every new phase in this progression gave marketers new storytelling capabilities. Sure, there will always be more traditional media opportunities that marketers want to buy, from the Olympic Games to the Super Bowl. But in many ways, the digital storytelling platform has turned the tables on the old broadcast media model.

Instead of vying for the best real estate and inserting my ad, hoping for the best, I am focused on reaching my target audience wherever they are, whenever they are there, 24 hours a day, seven days a week. I can target an audience that is hardwired to love my kind of story while not wasting money on those who don't. Essentially, I run my own ad network, aggregating target audiences in ways that are both free and paid. And I develop my own programming designed to tell the story of my brand and enable the 10-second customer journey. Even better, I know exactly what is and isn't working and can pivot my story on the fly, without having to wait around as precious dollars flow out and are wasted on content that doesn't cut it.

Just like with any media network, this reality has placed a premium on effective storytelling.

A digital storytelling platform is not merely a creative exercise or only about content development. It is not just about driving *audience* growth. It is a system that works together to drive *customer* growth. To do that, it's essential to have a clear growth objective in mind when developing your approach. How many times have you heard someone say, "I'm going to create a podcast/blog/video/ Instagram feed/webinar" without thinking about the underlying growth metrics and objectives? If it's just for fun, that's one thing, but in business, you are expected to show ROI for the work you do and the money you invest. Creating content is expensive, time consuming, and difficult to sustain, and that's before you start to build an audience around it.

But that doesn't mean it's impossible. Just ask Blake, aka GuerrillaZen.

The story of how I met Blake started with a problem. No matter how fit I am, it always seems like my belly is sticking out, and that really frustrates me. So, just like everyone trying to solve a problem, I turned to the internet and began searching for potential solutions to what I thought might be a posture problem. That led to the discovery of something called "anterior pelvic tilt," which is apparently very common today among people who spend a lot of time seated at a computer. Searching for "anterior pelvic tilt" set off the red flares of the digital ecosystem, announcing to the world that I was officially what you might call a "posture enthusiast." Lo and behold, one particular search result caught my eye: A YouTube video from Blake, owner of GuerrillaZen Fitness, on "How to fix anterior pelvic tilt." Of course, I watched it.

Shortly thereafter, I decided to start following Blake on Instagram, where he demonstrated all kinds of posture fixes through core strengthening and stretching. At some point, I read in his feed that he was offering a downloadable guide on "How to fix anterior pelvic tilt" on his website. So I went to his website, gave him my email address, and downloaded it. While on his site, I learned that Blake offered personal coaching sessions. Boom. I decided to move ahead, which led to a very fun video coaching session. I continue to follow him on Instagram to this day.

Blake's primary business model is coaching, and he uses his multi-part storytelling platform to identify and grow his customer base. To do this, he built a website, generated content for the site, created a streaming library on YouTube, and built a following on Instagram – a whopping 200,000-plus posture-loving followers.

My posture experience turned into a fun, real-life example about how the different components of the digital storytelling platform fed into my customer journey. While it may have taken more than ten seconds, the time from search to session was only about a week. And Blake is not a multi-billion-dollar corporation spending millions of dollars on advertising and digital infrastructure.

When I started at the AMA, it was clear that our story wasn't getting through to our current and prospective members. I shared the story of GuerrillaZen with my team and told them that if Blake could figure out how to maximize a digital storytelling platform, we could too. After all, we had plenty of valuable stories to tell. We just needed to get the platform in place.

At the AMA, our digital storytelling platform has been an important engine to help us achieve our highest levels of membership in 20 years. It also helped us reduce our reliance on direct mail by meeting our audience where they spend a ton of time: Online.

To help "package" (yes, that's purposeful) the strategy behind the AMA's storytelling approach, my Vice President (VP) of Digital, Ryan Wells, did what good marketers do. He came up with a name to explain it, called the "6-S" digital storytelling platform: Site, search, social, streaming, subscriptions, and spend. Each component has its own purpose and metrics, but they all work together to drive member growth and retention:

1. **Site**: The website itself is a "product" that needs to fit seamlessly with the other components of our customer experience – marketing, commerce, and service – to drive member growth. Having an ugly, unintuitive, friction-filled website is like having peeling paint on your home's exterior when you are trying to sell it. It makes the process of selling infinitely harder. Fortunately, we already had an excellent content team in place at the AMA, an outgrowth of a print-based news operation that was shuttered years earlier. But the original news content they produced, which generated most of our audience, was published on a separate website without any membership promotion at all. Essentially, we didn't have *a* marketing funnel. We had *two*. And the one with all the content, driving all the audience, was the one that didn't help drive membership, our ultimate goal.

   So, we changed that.

We re-envisioned the website as a dynamic content marketing platform built to expand top-of-the-funnel visitors and drive search engine discovery. Then we built the hooks throughout the site to convert visitors to members and re-built the underlying commerce platforms to minimize friction and ensure we captured the value of all portions of the customer journey.

Re-imagining our site and approach drove immediate results, which have continued to this day. We've increased the number of visitors to the site by more than 600% and now interact with the majority of our members and a significant portion of all physicians and medical students. And we know how driving audience translates to membership, and at what cost.

2. **Search**: In concert with the re-imagined site, we re-oriented our content marketing operation to drive organic search traffic – the kind that comes from people typing in search terms online, seeing us come up in a top position in search results, and clicking through to our site instead of someone else's.

    The goal was to appear on the first page of search results for the keywords that mattered the most to our audience. But even more specifically, we wanted to be one of the first three results the user would see. The value of being one of the "top results on the first page" is well known, and the approach to getting there is both scientific and consumer driven. We started by looking at the intersection between the content we were good at producing, the number of searches for that kind of content, and where we currently showed up in the search results. For example, we looked at the term "physician burnout," which is a central topic in our mission efforts to improve the lives of physicians. It became clear that something was wrong.

We ranked very poorly in search results – like, page 7 bad. Other content producers with a far smaller membership were performing much better.

A huge part of fixing the problem wasn't the content. It was our website infrastructure. The site needed to be built properly for search engine discovery, with articles properly tagged and loaded with the right keywords. In that regard, we treated Google and other search engines as some of our most important digital customers. The other solution: Creating content that answered the questions our audience was typing into search engines. We started delivering how-to articles by the dozens, geared to an enthusiast audience that couldn't get enough coverage of medicine, patient care, and the health care landscape. The result of all that work? Page 1, top three on Google search results.

3. **Social**: The story is currently being written on whether the rise of social media is a net win or loss for society. What's not up for debate is that its reach is massive. A DataReportal April 2023 global overview of social media data showed that social media growth continues, despite the increased warnings about its potential impact on overall health.[5] More than 150 million new users came online for the first time during the previous 12 months. Sixty percent of the global population uses social media. The average social media user spends nearly two-and-a-half hours on various platforms *every day*.

While we already had significant followers on social networks like Facebook and X (formerly Twitter) when

---

[5] "Digital 2023 April Global Statshot Report" in *DataReportal*, (2023, April 27). Available from: https://datareportal.com/reports/digital-2023-april-global-statshot [Accessed 13 February 2024].

I arrived at the AMA, these channels were being used primarily to distribute our news articles and press statements. This isn't to suggest that is a bad way to use those channels. But was it the only way to use those networks? Were physicians even using these platforms?

Following the lead from our new site and content marketing re-orientation, we began viewing social networks as storytelling and content marketing platforms. We put the pedal to the metal to increase our followers and social interactions even more. We continued to use the channels as a means to distribute our content, but we upped our content game with more powerful messaging and videos. As new social networks have grown in popularity, we've grown with them, adding YouTube, Instagram, TikTok and, most recently, Threads.

Adding a new social platform to the mix is not to be taken lightly. Each social platform has its own unique flavor, approach, and audience – not to mention constant updates to underlying algorithms. Keeping up with changes takes resources to manage effectively. So, we've been careful about which ones we add to the mix and walk before we run. But as long as our target audience flocks to social media channels, we will be there to share content and messaging that delivers value to our audience and helps us boost AMA membership.

4. **Streaming**: At the *Daily Racing Form*, I'd seen the power of adding low-cost video to our enthusiast-oriented content marketing operation. So powerful was this inexpensive form of content that we built a studio in a closet. We started producing programs with our top handicappers analyzing upcoming races and making their picks. Sometimes, we even left the closet and broadcast live from the track or an event.

There was clearly an opportunity to do something similar with low-cost video at the AMA. The inspiration came from an unlikely source: The COVID-19 pandemic. With a dearth of information on the pandemic and an acute need to communicate more with physicians, we started a daily video segment in the spring of 2020 called the "AMA Covid-19 Update." In it, we interviewed AMA leaders, as well as subject matter experts from inside and outside the AMA on a wide variety of COVID-19-related topics. This was all done remotely, captured initially via Microsoft Teams and Zoom.

The segments, which ran on our site and YouTube channel, became very popular among our audience. As the pandemic wore on, we became more sophisticated with what we produced and how we leveraged the content. For starters, we began posting a transcript of the video conversation on our site, scoring a win for search engine discoverability. Then, our reporters created more formal articles based on the videos, meaning even more discoverable content. After that, we turned the videos into podcasts for distribution on Spotify and Apple Podcasts. The podcast version allowed us to reach an entirely new audience while they worked out, went for socially distanced walks or commuted to their jobs. We posted the full videos to YouTube and created shorter versions for social platforms.

The bottom line? We turned one piece of content into many, fueling our storytelling platform. We adopted the mantra "COPE": Create once, publish everywhere.

Once we'd established a track record, we adapted a former photography studio into a full-fledged mini-production studio, upping our production values and capabilities. Three years and more than 700 episodes later, what is now the award-winning AMA Update continues to be a content engine and a powerful way to tell our story every day.

5. **Subscriptions**: Getting visitors to subscribe to newsletters and additional, ongoing communications provides an important way to increase engagement. I'm sure everyone recognizes at this point that if you buy something online, you're likely to begin receiving email communication from the retailer, even though you may have not actively signed up for it. A customer's email address is valuable, and well-used, it can lead to a continuing relationship and additional revenue. Unfortunately, companies often misuse email, leading customers to unsubscribe from future communications. This is a tremendous loss of value.

One of my recent 10-second customer journeys illustrates the cost of poor email use. Recently, I saw an Instagram ad for an exercise and training program run by a top Hollywood trainer. I signed up on a whim in ten seconds. As a fitness enthusiast, I would welcome more communication from this trainer with tips and additional insights to make me look like one of the "Chrises"' (Hemsworth, Evans, Pratt, in case you don't get the Hollywood reference). But instead, the first email I got was from the platform provider, suggesting a different course – on photography! It took me a minute to figure out why I'd even received the email in the first place, and once I did, it only took me a second to unsubscribe.

Remember: Enthusiast audiences have unlimited attention for the things which they are interested in, and no attention for what they're not. This means there are many options for increasing the number of subscriptions with your audience, as long as they deliver real value. Our main subscription newsletter at the AMA is a daily news digest email called Morning Rounds®, with hundreds of thousands of subscribers. We took a play from the *New York Times* and began to think about creating more content subscriptions for targeted areas of the site. We've done these in the form of browser alerts, which let the user know when new content they've subscribed to appears on the site. We have generated hundreds of thousands of additional subscriptions through this method, without clogging anyone's inbox. But we never assume that interest in one topic means that the subscriber is interested in something unrelated. That would be a fast path to "unsubscribe."

6. **Spend**: I mentioned earlier that running a content operation today is like being a broadcaster who builds an audience from both free and paid sources. Much of what we've discussed above is the result of organic traffic that comes to your site and content without spending money on paid search, digital ads, or social advertising. At one time, a company's social posts went out into the feeds of all their followers, which was a short-lived heaven for businesses.

But as time went on, social networks began to throttle back how many of your followers received those messages for free and shifted to a paid distribution model. That meant organic reach had to be complemented by paid campaigns to reach the same audience that, in those golden years of early Facebook, was free. In today's environment, if you want to reach your full social audience, including your followers on social media, you'll need to spend money.

The good news is that if your 6-S platform is working together, your marketing spend will be efficient and well-targeted. With careful tracking and measurement, you can ensure that your dollars are driving growth.

The mix of what you spend your budget on varies by business. There are some businesses – say, for example, in travel – that spend tens (or hundreds) of millions of dollars in paid search, with a highly scientific understanding of what keywords drive conversion and revenue. For the AMA, there are high-intent search terms we buy to drive traffic to our most compelling content.

Sometimes, paying to "boost" content on social media can be a more effective storytelling approach than buying a standard digital ad. One of the benefits of a high-functioning 6-S operation, with a robust subscription operation, is the ability to turn email addresses into "custom audiences" with social networks. This allows you to pay for and reach only the people you want and avoid spending money on people far less likely to become or remain customers.

While this 6-S model currently works for organizations and individuals now, what about the future? This model relies on using content to drive traffic to your site. It's possible that ChatGPT or other AI-powered search engines will throw a big wrench into the works by answering customer questions before they ever get to your site. It is too early to tell how this will evolve over time, but there is the potential for a seismic shift in digital marketing strategy. Be ready.

***

Your story is solid, and your 6-S digital storytelling platform is in place. You are ready to tell the world about your game-changing new product that solves a key pain point for your target customer. Now, the rubber hits the road in the 10-second customer journey: The commerce transaction.

As you probably know from your own experience, this step is tricky. One glitch in the commerce path, and boom, the customer abandons ship. Don't let all the time you've spent guiding your customer through the tornado funnel go to waste at the last moment. Let's talk next about how you can apply the full force of friction-reduction in the commerce process.

Chapter 7

#FYCOP (Fix your checkout page)

I'm sure this scenario has happened to you a million times: You decide to pull the trigger on a purchase, and as you head through checkout, something goes awry. Maybe the site you're buying from doesn't look secure or trustworthy, your promo code doesn't work, or your credit card is declined for no apparent reason. So, you "abandon your cart" and never come back.

Would it shock you to know that the average rate of shopping cart abandonment – where people don't complete their online shopping transaction – is about 70%?[1]

That's a pretty stunning statistic. Losing a customer in the digital commerce process is especially frustrating given how much work you put into getting them there in the first place. No matter how much friction you remove in the journey – the right targeting,

---

[1] Baymard Institute, 2023 shopping cart abandonment statistics. Available from: https://baymard.com/lists/cart-abandonment-rate [Accessed 13 February 2024].

a compelling brand proposition, an outstanding product, and a storytelling platform that brought the customer to your site – one misstep at this stage can be the end of the road.

Stamping out friction is one of the most important roles of a CXO. In fact, the CXO could very reasonably be renamed the Chief Friction-Reduction Officer. And nowhere is it more important to stamp out friction than the moment you're about to close the deal.

Amazon has shown the world what frictionless commerce looks like. They took "customer-centric" and turned it into "customer-obsessed." You might not agree with all their tactics, but the reality is that if you want to truly compete and excel on the 10-second customer journey, being like Amazon (or any of the other digital commerce giants who have followed its lead) is the bar to clear for entry into the game of excellence.

I am by no means the world's e-commerce expert. If you were looking for a "How to beat Amazon at its own game" chapter in this book, I apologize. I don't have the answer for that. Neither does anyone else right now. The best we've got is, "If you can't beat 'em, learn from 'em."

But what I do have is experience, having seen and extinguished my fair share of commerce friction across many different businesses. In this chapter, I'll share some of my friction-fighting approaches and what I've learned from some folks who are way smarter than I am.

***

Sometimes, the best advice is the simplest. I was reminded of this at a recent dinner with Patrick and John Collison, co-founders of the incredibly successful payment platform company Stripe. Launched in September 2011 as a payment processing software for businesses, the company hit the $1 billion valuation mark just three years later. By early 2023, the company was valued at more than $50 billion.[2] It serves more than 3.1 million active websites for businesses based in 46 countries.[3]

I told the Collison brothers I was writing a book and asked for their advice on how to reduce commerce friction. I was blown away by the simplicity and clarity of Patrick's response: "Reduce the complexity of your checkout page."

Patrick told the story of how they had recently done testing on their own checkout page. The first developer to take the challenge ran an experiment that produced a 7% improvement in conversion. Somewhat skeptical of the magnitude of this win, they asked a second person to give it a try, building off the learning from the first round. This developer produced an 11% improvement.

Patrick asked: "What would you be willing to pay for an 11% lift in conversion on your checkout page? Probably a lot, right? Start by just fixing your checkout page."

His story resonated with me in a number of ways. First, this is a guy who is clearly brilliant and wildly successful. But his advice centered around one of the key concepts in this book: Experimentation and data-driven testing (that's coming up in Chapter 8).

Second, it speaks to the benefit of teaming up with partners who are doing the hard work of optimization. Think of it this way: Literally tens of thousands of companies across the country rely on Stripe for their payment and subscription platform,

---

[2] Available from: https://cnbc.com/2023/03/15/stripe-raises-series-i-billion-at-sharply-reduced-50-billion-valuation.html?qsearchterm=stripe%20raises%20series%20i%20billio%20at%20sharply%20reduced [Accessed 13 February 2024].

[3] Available from: https://backlinko.com/stripe-users [Accessed 13 February 2024].

including their checkout design. Wouldn't it be nice for them to have someone else figure out how to boost your checkout page conversions by more than 10%?

So, here's your first marching order: Simplify your checkout page. More broadly, look closely at all your other key "conversion" pages with the same lens. One of my team's recent discoveries reminded me just how important this is.

At the AMA, we created a research tool that helps medical students determine which residency programs are the best fit for them. While this research tool is available to all medical students, there is a premium feature available only to members. This premium feature is valuable enough that it drives a lot of medical students to join the AMA. Because the research tool has been around for many years, we have a pretty good benchmark on how many student memberships it will generate. But this year, we noticed that something was off: The number of members generated by this important application was down significantly year-over-year. We dug in to figure out why. Turns out the premium feature link that allows a student to upgrade was broken.

Ouch.

We got that problem fixed in a few days and turned the situation around. But the fact that no one caught it sooner was a wakeup call for all of us. We were so focused on adding a lot of new features to the application that we weren't paying attention to the one thing that made the biggest difference.

The Collison brothers' advice inspired me to create a joke hashtag for my team, #fycop for "fix your checkout page." This hashtag reminds them to stay focused on the pages that matter the most, with constant testing to improve results.

Finding problems like this can be frustrating. Rather than dwell on the past, I decided it's much better to celebrate discoveries like this and continue to look forward.

Just like the straightforward #fycop directive, addressing commerce friction is not about being Amazon-level brilliant. It's about having a set of tools and approaches that do most of the blocking and tackling for you.

Here are my top ten friction-fighting approaches:

1. **A/B testing**: Just as the example with Stripe illustrated, A/B testing is a miracle tool. We live in an amazing age when you can constantly and systematically experiment with changes to your e-commerce platform to turn more potential customers into actual customers. Test and track everything in your funnel. Yes, everything. And remember, this is not a "set it and forget it" thing. Have someone always watching to ensure that nothing goes awry in your key conversion benchmarks. If you see a change, dig in.

2. **Call-to-Action (CTA)**: Make it easy for customers to act. I am constantly amazed when I visit landing pages and literally can't find the "buy" option. Sometimes it is stuck all the way at the bottom of the page where no one will get to. I'm not suggesting you be the digital version of a carnival barker, but you don't want to be shy about spurring potential customers to action. Put your CTA throughout all your key conversion pages. And make sure you're focused on the key action. Having too many unrelated CTAs on a page can distract a customer from the one that matters the most.

3. **Subscriptions**: If it feels like every site wants you to start subscribing to a product immediately, it's because they do. And with good reason. Recurring revenue is an important benchmark and subscriptions are a key retention tool. Amazon's Subscribe-&-Save is a great example of this in the e-commerce world. Subscribing allows customers to save money on products they use regularly and helps

them be sure there is a predictable supply arriving on the doorstep when they need it. On the flip side, asking a brand-new customer to commit to a subscription for an unfamiliar product can create friction. How to figure out the right approach? See #1 (A/B testing) above.

4. **Auto renewal**: Auto renewal is the key to retention for subscriptions, including memberships. The more people you can get on auto renewal, the better. And it's generally a win–win. The seller retains more customers and reduces marketing costs. The buyer doesn't need to worry about an expiration date, especially on things where continuity is important. For example, when our children were born, we elected to store some of the umbilical cord blood, with the idea that it could be helpful should they experience a serious medical condition later in life. I didn't want to worry about that subscription lapsing, so I made sure the payment was on auto renewal.

5. **Credit card checks**: You know what most frequently turns auto renewals into something other than recurring revenue? Failed credit cards. Credit cards expire, and I'll go out on a limb and say that doesn't just happen on the same day as the subscription auto renews. Don't wait until a subscription ends to check the validity of the credit card. Use a service to ensure that the credit card on file is in working order well in advance, and if it isn't, begin a campaign to encourage an update before it's too late.

6. **The digital ad "handoff"**: You've placed a social media ad that offers your T-shirt in a hot new blue color. Your potential customer clicks on that ad and lands on a page with the item in brown – or, worse, a homepage filled with hundreds of items other than what they were looking for. The handoff between an ad and website is as crucial as that between a quarterback and running back. Make it seamless and in line with your potential customer's expectations.

7. **Login**: Digital security is a good thing. Login problems are not. There was a time at the AMA when login issues drove a big chunk of our customer service contacts. People are inundated with requests to create usernames and passwords, and there are requirements that force them to make each different from their other passwords. At the AMA, we're required to verify that people are physicians when they sign up for membership. That made it incumbent upon us to make the process incredibly easy. For normal login procedures, there are lots of ways to make this smoother, including "social sign-on" (validating identity through their existing social or commerce platform logins) and automated password recovery. For commerce transactions, you can never sacrifice security for ease. But it's important to consider whether you need someone to log in to make a purchase or not. This step can be the proverbial straw that broke the journey, driving a customer away at the last moment. This is why "guest checkout" and one-click payment approaches like Apple Pay are such important options to offer.

8. **Upsells**: There is a rule in sales: When someone says, "Yes," stop talking. The same holds true with commerce. Unless your testing shows otherwise, don't interrupt customers with other product offers until after the deal is done. Make the sale, put a smile on your customer's face, *then* worry about upsell offers. Even then, make sure the offer makes sense in the context of the purchase. Recently, when I was about to complete a purchase, I was offered the "opportunity" to buy the same product at the same price. Why would I do that?

9. **Email**: A customer's email address is gold. Treat it like that. Don't let the first thing you do with a new customer's email address be to spam them with impersonalized, ceaseless email communication. This is the quickest way to

an "unsubscribe" and a loss of the ability to communicate in the future. Be patient and use the tools available to you to determine how often to communicate with new customers and about what. Compare three examples coming out of my recent purchases. One company started sending me daily emails about their entire product line and sales immediately, before I even received what I bought. In less than a week, I'd unsubscribed. On the other hand, my favorite clothing brand Suitsupply sent me an immediate follow-up email with related merchandise that would complement the item I just bought, sent from the sales associate I'd worked with in the store. Score. The third company started sending me bi-weekly emails after a couple of weeks, not trying to sell me anything (it was already a subscription). Instead, the email addressed topics related to my health and fitness activities, kind of like they knew me. I actually look forward to reading their emails. If you can make your customer feel like that, you're doing something right.

10. **Accessibility**: The internet has become an essential tool for people of all ages and abilities. But many of those folks face significant challenges when trying to use websites. It is important to optimize your website's design for those with eyesight and hearing difficulties. Consider these statistics from a Statista report:

   a. 75% of adults 65 and older use the internet.[4]
   b. An estimated 300 million people around the world have color vision deficiency.[5]

---

[4] Available from: www.usnews.com/360-reviews/services/senior-tech-aging-in-place-survey#:~:text=About%2075%25%20of%20adults%20 65,to%20the%20Pew%20Research%20Center [Accessed 13 February 2024].

[5] Available from: www.colourblindawareness.org/colour-blindness/ [Accessed 13 February 2024].

c. Nearly 5% of U.S. adults have a vision disability with blindness or serious difficulty seeing, even when wearing glasses.[6]

d. Nearly 6% of U.S. adults are deaf or have serious difficulty hearing.[7]

e. More than 6 in 10 adults with a disability own a laptop or desktop computer, and more than 7 in 10 own a smartphone.[8]

Despite those numbers, 96.8% of homepages had detectable failures in Web Content Accessibility 2.0 Guidelines.[9] The most common problems were low-contrast text, missing alternative text, empty links, missing form input labels, empty buttons, and missing document language. It's not just businesses that are failing here. More than 90% of the most popular federal websites failed to meet the standards for accessibility, according to a recent Information Technology and Innovation Study. In total, 90% of websites are inaccessible to people with disabilities who use assistive technologies.

Understanding, identifying, and addressing accessibility issues can be a challenge. Working with a skilled outside partner, like we're doing at the AMA, is a great way to make fast, consistent progress no matter how big the punch list is.

---

[6] Available from: https://www.cdc.gov/ncbddd/disabilityandhealth/infographic-disability-impacts-all.html [Accessed 13 February 2024].

[7] Available from: https://www.cdc.gov/ncbddd/disabilityandhealth/infographic-disability-impacts-all.html [Accessed 13 February 2024].

[8] Available from: www.pewresearch.org/short-reads/2021/09/10/americans-with-disabilities-less-likely-than-those-without-to-own-some-digital-devices/ [Accessed 13 February 2024].

[9] Available from: www.boia.org/blog/despite-new-doj-guidance-many-organizations-havent-adopted-accessible-web-design [Accessed 13 February 2024].

So, whose responsibility is it to ensure a frictionless commerce experience for your customers? I think it's a copout to say, "It's everyone's job," just like it is the marketing kiss of death to say that your target audience is everybody. Many people within an organization have a role in helping create a friction-free customer experience and helping master the tornado funnel. But in today's digital environment, it's important that someone – ideally the CXO – takes the lead and hopefully has the authority to be the Chief Friction-Reduction Officer. This is especially important because a lot of what creates customer friction isn't "owned" by a particular business unit within an organization, and so there's not necessarily someone to pick up the ball and run with it. Bruce Temkin, a key CX thought leader and former Head of the Qualtrics XM Institute recognized that customer experience problems often emanate from spaces in organizations no one "owns" or processes and that people aren't empowered to change. This observation resonated with me as my team has stepped up to "own" capabilities that cut across multiple parts of the organization.

Typical commerce problems like the ones we've discussed in this chapter fit that bill, as root cause issues often cut across marketing, IT, and customer service. This kind of friction can literally cost you – back to the "fix your checkout page" example. It is sometimes easier to get attention around solving problems with a big pay-off, but even then, it requires leadership, results-focused collaboration, and teamwork.

This is another reason why CX and marketing are organizational soulmates, and why, for our organization, having CX be part of the marketing team makes the most sense. This partnership is essential to getting the job done. But, in addition, these two teams are often best equipped to generate the data that shows how customer experience initiatives translate to growth. And in today's digital age, it's all about, yes, the data.

Let's talk about what you need to do to be in the best position to generate and use all that data.

Chapter 8
Developing a test-and-learn culture

Much like the video gamers we talked about in a previous chapter, I'm a very competitive person.

I constantly push myself to beat results or do things in less time, from weightlifting to my morning coffee routine. This sense of competitiveness even extends to my daily commute into downtown Chicago. I'm always looking for a better, shorter way.

I'm certain I'm not alone here. When you make the same trip every day, you accumulate a lot of data, from how long things should take to what routes to avoid and shortcuts to take. You occasionally try new routes to see if you can beat the old results. Sometimes, this is not by choice, but by circumstances. A few months ago, construction on the typical route to my Chicago office encouraged me to travel one more exit and enter the scary, Gotham City-like underground road in Chicago called Lower Wacker Drive (this stretch of underground road was actually the set for The Dark Knight Rises, so I'm not imagining the resemblance). Turns out that this route, while technically longer in distance, shaved five minutes off my commute. I was delighted by the surprise discovery.

In other words, on a commute like this, you have:

- A lot of data over time.

- A benchmark for what constitutes normal outcomes.

- A literal dashboard to measure progress.

- A testing plan that lets you optimize results.

- A clear objective: Reduce commuting time.

This commuting example provides a reasonable analogy for how we think about and measure customer experience, where millions of transactions of all kinds allow us to create performance benchmarks and daily dashboards to measure progress. And with a proper testing mentality and plan – and the latest in "voice-of-the-customer" tools – you can systematically use this data to crush customer friction and drive growth.

Notice the order of operations in that previous sentence. First you create the proper testing mentality, then you come up with the plan. Without the right mindset among the members of your team, all that data you're about to bring in is just meaningless facts and figures. If there isn't a culture of testing and a reliance on data for decisions, then friction will continue to thwart your efforts at customer experience.

How do you build a data-driven testing culture, and what does it look like when you actually have one? A data-driven testing culture looks more like a science lab than a creative agency. It is based on the scientific method:

1. Question

2. Research

3. Hypothesis

4. Experiment

5. Data Analysis

6. Conclusion

The process repeats itself with each new problem or opportunity. That's what a data-driven test-and-learn culture looks like. Not what you see in your organization? That's not surprising. The scientific, data-driven, test-and-learn mentality is not necessarily second nature to traditional marketing organizations. But keeping up with the demands of the 10-second customer journey requires a mentality shift. The inspiration for mine came from a very unlikely place. You might say, in fact, that it was a spiritual awakening.

***

When I turned 50, I realized that nearly a decade of commuting to Manhattan and years of working in the New York digital media world had turned me into a short-tempered stress ball. At the encouragement of my wife, I decided to make a change and enroll in a transcendental meditation course. And while I found the training to be a bit wacky, the practice of meditating, which I did back and forth on my 45-minute train ride, proved to be transformational (Google "NYT how to meditate on your commute" and you'll find a photo of me and my friend Adam meditating on our commute into Manhattan from New Jersey).

At about the same time, something else happened that had an equal impact on my brain and outlook: The invention of easy, digital A/B testing.

There was a time when people would spend hour after hour arguing about what would work and what wouldn't work without any real way to resolve creative differences. Then they would plow ahead with whatever option was deemed best. This was the era in which creative directors at ad agencies reigned supreme. Whatever these folks said was gospel, and your job was to accept their opinion and execute the campaign according to their untested wisdom. If that meant making the ketchup bottle tiny and sticking it in the corner of the ad where no one would see it, so be it.

Sometimes, a different person – maybe a client – would come up with a zany idea at which even the creative director would raise an eyebrow. Then, it would devolve into a battle of opinions about which way to proceed, with big stakes. This dynamic felt a lot like the frustration and stress I experienced on my commutes, where there was very little that I could do to make the train go faster.

A/B testing changed all that. Put simply, A/B testing is a head-to-head digital experiment that, with a relative degree of scientific certainty, determines which options or approaches are better. Prior to the last decade, it was extremely difficult and time consuming to run A/B tests. You used to have to build two alternative paths using your team's precious development and production resources and manually direct traffic to different options.

Then, Optimizely came on the scene and changed everything.

Optimizely was founded in 2010 by Dan Siroker and Pete Koomen, both formerly of Google. In 2013, it was recognized as a finalist for the Digital Analytics Association New Technology of the Year Awards for Excellence, and Siroker was named in the Forbes 30 Under 30 list.

And with good reason. The company's software-as-a-service offering allowed marketing teams to conduct constant, inexpensive A/B tests to hone designs, optimize conversion rates, increase click-through rates, or deliver whatever metric that mattered most. Suddenly, you could make changes to your website on the fly and easily route a certain percentage of your audience to two different places. Each would see a different color palette, a button placed in a different spot or differently worded copy, all without using any development resources at all. Once you started the experiment, user traffic would be distributed randomly and evenly across the two alternatives. For a digital marketer, this was the equivalent of a miracle.

My colleague Jordan at the *Daily Racing Form* and I used to joke that we were running so many A/B tests, no one knew what the website actually looked like except us. We started deploying these experiments all the way through the marketing funnel to optimize our campaigns and conversions, even employing an outside firm to help us develop and prioritize tests that would deliver the biggest bang for the buck. Whether it was a piece of content or something as subtle as the color of a button on the website, suddenly we could get nearly real-time feedback from our target audience that allowed us to make better decisions every day.

Turns out that A/B testing and transcendental meditation had a lot in common. They both rewired my brain, improved my outlook, increased my creativity, and led to a much calmer and more focused existence. The reason is simple: A/B testing made it much safer to test ideas before unleashing a campaign or site change to the masses. It changed the conversation around the table from opinion to fact. It also enabled me to start building a culture of on-the-fly learning and experimentation wherever my career took me.

There were some other unexpected side effects, including:

- **Increased humility**: It can be incredibly and necessarily humbling to see things repeatedly turn out in ways you don't expect. Of course, it's also incredibly liberating to know you don't have to be right all the time, and the stakes are low for experiments.

- **Loss of appetite**: Not for food, though, but for the question "Why?" as A/B testing makes the question unnecessary because the results give you the answer. Why are we doing this? Because the data shows it works.

That doesn't mean you necessarily know why something works. There may never be a logical reason as to why your audience prefers the blue button vs. the red button. But you choose the blue button because it enables you to hit the metric(s) that matters most. That's why.

- **Decreased agitation**: A/B testing means you don't have to pull your hair out every single time a colleague or senior manager comes up with some kooky idea or disagrees with your opinion. Just run the test and prove that the idea is kooky, not because you said so but because the test said so. A/B testing doesn't put an end to ideas and opinions; it is your ticket out of those endless opinion-based arguments. Oh, and by the way, maybe their kooky idea is actually great. (See #1 above.)

- **Improvement cravings**: Once you start with A/B testing, it's hard to stop. Oh, sure, you can say you could stop, but why would you want to stop improving things? In this world, 5% improvement in anything is like a major shot of business adrenaline, and you'll crave more ideas and hypotheses to test.

- **Constant optimization syndrome**: Your love of A/B testing might creep into your non-digital life. Everything becomes a test, from identifying the right seat on the subway to finding the best way to get your daughter to clean her room.

More than a decade after Optimizely changed A/B testing, I still use it at the AMA. The team that helped us design our experiments at the *Daily Racing Form* has moved on to something new and exciting (more on that later), but that moment in time changed me dramatically. I went from being a guesser and someone who openly resisted what I thought were crazy ideas to an experimenter and a person who was willing to give just about anything an A/B test to search for the truth. I never looked back.

But I realized something else in that moment that truly changed me forever: A/B testing isn't just about testing. It's about creating a new culture where safe, low-cost experimentation drives better business results. It wasn't enough for *me* to be an experimenter. I needed to create a test-and-learn culture throughout the organization, one in which individuals were encouraged and enabled to routinely examine every single opportunity to see if a better way can be found. Check your egos at the door. This is about the data.

When I arrived at the AMA, I had a pretty strong hunch that our email program was not working as well as it could. I had no actionable data to determine whether it was the format and design of the email template, the subject lines, the placement of CTA buttons, or the content itself. All I knew was that there appeared to be a tremendous amount of potential upside if we could figure out how to do email marketing more effectively.

So, I rolled up my sleeves and worked with a designer to re-do the email template. I started working with the writing team to test alternate subject line approaches and placement of membership CTAs every time we sent an email.

Lo and behold, the tests began identifying exactly what we could do to improve the most coveted metrics: Member generation and retention. It wasn't about what I, someone without any experience in the health care industry thought, nor about what some long-tenured creative director believed should be done to improve performance.

It was about the data.

Marketing is a combination of art and science in which the creative types are often extremely wary of the science part. Testing makes the science part less scary. It's a way to prove that a creative person's most inspired work moves the needle on growth.

Once the team members got a taste of testing, they fell in love with it too. Our test-and-learn culture was off and running, and every win created a sense of momentum and optimism. We leaned on this new test-and-learn culture for more and more things – our websites, our ads, you name it. Pretty soon, testing and learning wasn't just something we did. It was who we were as a team.

On the way, I've learned three important guard rails about building a test-and-learn culture:

1. **Keep your eye on the real metric.** The end goal is customer growth. With A/B testing, it's easy to lose track of what matters as you become fascinated by intermediary improvements. Wow, the green button drives 10% more clicks than the red button! But does that improvement drive more sales or convert more customers in the end? It is important to follow the test all the way to the end because some intermediary changes don't make a difference.

2. **Ensure the testing culture doesn't break down, especially as people enter and exit an organization.** A company's culture is the sum of the beliefs, opinions, and attitudes of the people in it. In any business, those people are going to change. People come and people go. Your job as a CXO is to make sure that the test-and-learn culture stays intact and that the learning isn't lost when people leave. It also means hiring the right kind of people who find this environment motivating. Look for those who show curiosity and a demonstrated history of relying on data to determine what works. These are the type of people who can't resist hitting "enter" repeatedly to update a dashboard, sales, or subscription report. They can't stop looking at Google Analytics because they get such a charge from seeing the numbers grow. I call them "people who like the sound of the cash register ringing."

3. **Promote successes by having teams present their experiments and results to wider audiences.** Ideally,

a test-and-learn culture will reduce the role of egos in a marketing department – the "humility" effect – and spur a hunger for further learning. One way to keep your test-and-learn culture vibrant is to allow teams to present their findings to a much wider audience. People like sharing their success stories and appreciate it when their gut feelings are confirmed by data. They even like showing what they learned when their experiments didn't work. Create a venue that allows them to share those stories, backed by data, and you'll see the energy and cohesion it creates.

***

Sometimes, it is amazing how many of the "old-school" lessons of the past we forget.

In writing this chapter about creating a test-and-learn culture and thinking about how to be a better data evangelist, I remembered an important marker of the data-driven culture at P&G. When I worked there in the 1980s, there were many, somewhat nerdy, but highly effective approaches that supported data-driven thinking. One of the most important was the "factbook."

If you were a brand management type at P&G, you had to be prepared to answer questions about the business on the spot. Senior leaders expected you to be able to cite historical market share figures and critical research learnings. Being in command of the data instilled confidence in your ability to steer the brand and business. With this approach, facts replaced opinions, conjecture, or lack of recall wherever possible. Now, there's a lot to know about a business, so no one expected you to pull out last year's Q3 market share differential between Scope Mouthwash and Listerine out of a hat. Instead, you opened your factbook binder filled with the most important data on the business, flipped to the tab about market share, and pulled the number. A key part of the job was adding to and culling from the factbook to make sure you were prepared for whatever question arose. Think of it as "business data curation."

In the digital age, it is very retro to think about carrying around a physical binder filled with printed documents. But this approach worked, and frankly, it offers a much better solution than keeping scattered, fact-filled documents on my desk or in files. I'm not recommending that you go out and buy binders for your team and ask them to start printing. But as part of building a test-and-learn, data-driven culture, you should expect your team to have quick access to the critical facts about how the business is performing.

Dashboards are today's equivalent of a factbook. The dashboard distills and tracks key metrics on one page. This ensures that your direct reports and all of their team members always have a top-level view of the business in comparison to (at least) last year.

Having dashboards for each element of the business is essential to staying on track. Dashboards also allow you to identify any deviations that might signal a problem and make the appropriate course corrections. Knowing when to hit the figurative alarm button is critical to preventing a bad day or week from turning into a bad year.

On my team at the AMA, we use dashboards to keep the various parts of the team on the same page regarding the health of the business. We review them weekly. We track our progress across all key metrics including:

- Marketing campaigns: Traffic, conversions, cost-per-acquisition, or cost-per-user (CPA/CPU).
- Membership: Results by audience segment vs. prior year.
- Digital audience: Results in total and by key traffic areas, tracked throughout the month and by month vs. prior year.
- SEO: Top search terms this week.
- Lead generation: How many leads our institutional marketing campaigns are generating by event or campaign.

All of these metrics are essential inputs into our marketing funnel, so it's critical that we understand any deviations that could affect the growth engine.

***

Now you know why building a test-and-learn culture is such an important part of the playbook: Because it can drive a company culture that values and celebrates growth and the elimination of customer friction. And I've shared with you some of my key approaches for this part of the CXO role.

Sharing the results of testing and research with the rest of your organization drives alignment and customer-focused action. Given the benefits, why doesn't this happen more frequently in organizations?

From my experience, I think it's a "What happens in Vegas stays in Vegas" problem: The learning generated in the marketing department stays in the marketing department. The data doesn't necessarily make its way out to the other parts of the organization, including the other X areas – product, commerce, and service. And it doesn't make its way down to all the folks doing the work, even in the marketing department itself. While some of the public-facing work of the marketing department (like advertising) is often very visible to the rest of the organization, the data and testing on which that work is based is often not widely shared. Neither are the amazing outcomes that friction-reduction efforts produce.

In other words, it's easy to make the mistake we discussed earlier in the book: To spend all the time on the product (in this case, the data or research) and not enough time on the marketing (communication to the rest of the organization). There are several reasons why this happens.

First, being a customer data evangelist takes a lot of time. Even in my relatively small organization of about 1,000 people, there isn't a venue where I can reach most or all the folks who would benefit. Sharing an important piece of customer research or testing means going on a road show across the organization, both up and down. There is a lot of legwork to go from the senior management team to department owners and to business owners and subject matter experts across multiple business units. And that takes a ton of time. My advice: Make time.

Second, sometimes being a data evangelist means having to share bad news with certain groups or about certain initiatives. It's never fun to share bad news, but it is necessary to get everyone on the same page and spur constructive action. Candor and transparency with data can at least help others understand the "why" even if the news is disappointing.

Third, not everyone sees the relevance of the research or data analysis that you are so excited about sharing. People across an organization are, not surprisingly, just doing their jobs. However fascinating your data is, folks in different departments or at different levels might not fully understand the implications of the data or have the ability to shift their work or priorities based on what you show them. So, manage your expectations about translating the learning into action.

Given these constraints, put a stake in the ground and prioritize your data evangelism by audience and venue. Stock every meeting with "data snacks." And identify the key pieces of research or data that you want everyone to know. In my current role, membership is the most visible and important metric, and it is shared widely on a monthly basis throughout the organization. That makes it critical that we have our factbook ready and are prepared to "get to why" on a real-time basis.

The trick to becoming an effective data evangelist relies on these five skills:

1. **Brevity**: We talked about the importance of brevity earlier regarding your brand proposition. Similarly, when

it comes to being a good data evangelist, it's critical to get to the point. Your internal company audience has a limited attention span, just like your customer audience. At P&G, there was another "old-school" approach to deal with this: The "one-page memo." Literally, you had to summarize every research or major brand initiative on a single page. The one-page format was fixed. It started with the recommendation, then moved to conclusions and specific findings before closing with the next steps. Distilling the story was not easy. In those days, we used typewriters and made corrections with White-Out! But the format works. Have you ever sat in a presentation that flows in just the opposite order? It makes me want to hyperventilate!

2. **Bite, snack, meal**: I borrowed this term from our content marketing team. The term guides their approach breaking up big pieces of content, like a 100-page report (a meal) into smaller, more digestible chunks appropriate for web publishing, like a three-page downloadable summary (snack) or an article (bite). The same goes for sharing data. You rarely get an hour with your CEO or senior-level colleagues to take them through an entire research report or business summary. So, be prepared to present smaller portions in meetings or even on the fly. Sharing a constant stream of interesting test or research "bites" helps spread the reach of a data-driven culture.

3. **Tell a story**: The ability to tell a logical, captivating story with data is an acquired skill. For that, I am forever indebted to my boss at Leo Burnett, Brad Brinegar, for teaching me how to tell a great data story, even in a PowerPoint deck. This once involved hearing the somewhat painful feedback that my presentation style was "aloof." But that feedback and other lessons showed me how to be more engaging and build a logical flow

that supported my conclusions. One of the key lessons: Label each slide with the conclusion you want your audience to reach, and make sure the slide supports the conclusion. You'd be amazed at how many presentations I see where the header of the slide is just the chart name, like "Membership Trends." I recently gave this advice to a team at the AMA and told them that I often start drafting a presentation with just the header statements to ensure there is a logical story flow.

4. **Visualize**: Make it easy for your audience to understand and engage. For many people, seeing the data come to life in a graphic is far more effective and persuasive than yet another chart. Recently, my team and I created a presentation that tracked changes in the physician landscape. The presentation started with a color-coded pie graph and followed with analyses of each slice of the pie. This approach took what could have been a very complicated and boring data story and made it interesting and easy to digest.

5. **Get to why**: The numbers alone just tell the "what." You and your team always need to understand the "why." Sometimes that comes through further analysis. But if that doesn't do the trick, I encourage you to use another old-school approach: Look at what you're doing. And I mean, literally, look at it. A while back, we were attempting to figure out some negative trends in our direct mail results. As part of the analysis, I asked the team to take over a conference room and post three years of direct mail pieces and emails on the wall, organized by month. Yes, this involved a lot of printing and taping. But seeing the work this way allowed us to detect a pattern in messaging and design that wasn't visible from just the numbers.

***

Before I started at the AMA, I thought about "test-and-learn" narrowly as a marketing approach. But now I see how this mentality connects to and powers the broader X of customer experience.

But testing alone isn't enough. Testing often doesn't give you the *why* behind customer experience issues or provide an ongoing framework for evaluating friction or measuring customer experience. And while testing might be able to identify a problem, getting it fixed is another story – especially when the problem falls in between different groups, without a clear owner.

That's why a new class of friction fighters has emerged in organizations. They've developed a new set of approaches, tools, and metrics for measuring customer experience under the banner of "CX."

Chapter 9
CX marks the spot

With the test-and-learn culture foundation under our belt, it's time to switch gears to another data-driven approach to fighting customer friction. It's called "CX."

Wait, isn't this whole book about customer experience? Isn't CX just the abbreviation?

Yes, it is confusing. It took me a while to wrap my head around it. Let me take a shot at explaining because it's important for you to know about the role that CX plays in driving the 10-second customer journey.

You might recall at the beginning of the book when I said that there has been a transition from "customer experience," the all-encompassing, every-touchpoint, concept to the zippier "CX." I think the reality is that it is more than an abbreviation. Essentially, efforts to quantify the value of customer experience and tie it to business results led to the development of CX, the discipline. Over the last twenty years, CX practitioners and consultants have developed a number of frameworks and best practices, including the well-known measure Net Promoter Score.

More importantly, a new class of friction fighters has emerged. They use a wide variety of tools like customer journey maps, blueprints, and data-based analytic tools to measure, predict, and avoid customer friction. To me, CX is a discipline on the level of marketing or product development. CX is a necessary, but not sufficient, component of overall customer experience.

So, what exactly does CX look like in action? How is it different to customer service? This chapter will answer those questions, starting with an overview of why and how we built the AMA's CX operation from the ground up. Then, we'll look at the key metrics of a CX operation, as well as examine some important organizational considerations.

***

When I first started at the AMA, we had an excellent customer service team and leader. But we did not have an enterprise-level customer experience strategy or CX operation. Honestly, I wasn't quite sure what the difference was at the time. But listening to our customers, talking to our team, and looking at the data showed a big opportunity to think differently about our approach.

Our customer service team was intensely focused on helping AMA members and customers do what they were trying to do, whether that was join the AMA or renew their membership, log onto the website to download content, buy a book, or even register a complaint. Over the course of time, customer needs became reasonably predictable and repetitive. Our team focused on how to address customer problems most efficiently, trying to solve their problems on the first contact and avoid channel switching, where a customer had to follow up with a phone call or email after they were unable to solve a problem online.

The customer service team was very good at this job. As a result, they earned recognition as one of the top 10% leading contact centers in the nation.

But our customer service paradigm was about optimizing within a broken system. While the team got very good at fixing customer problems on the spot (a model typically called "break-fix"), they had no ability to solve the underlying problems that generated customer contacts in the first place. Imagine how frustrating that would feel.

Here's an example. Every day, the team would get a sizeable number of calls from members having trouble logging in to our website. This "login problem" was well known and had been happening for a long time. The team was good at addressing it, using directions like "clear your cache" or re-setting the customer's password on the spot. While workarounds like this fixed the acute problem, the login problem itself persisted. (By the way, if you ever want to see steam come out of my ears, just tell me to "clear my cache.")

The bottom line was that customer issues with our login generated a whopping number and percentage of contacts to our service center. And physicians simply face too much administrative burden already for us to pile on.

Beyond the time and frustration involved, it was essential that our members – very busy physicians and medical students – be able to log onto the site. From a customer perspective, people expect to be able to handle basic tasks online, and if they can't log in, that's an enormous obstacle on the 10-second customer journey. From a marketing perspective, a login helped us understand who was a physician and who was a member of the general public. This kind of basic identification allowed us to target our audience properly and provide more personalized communications.

So, why did problems with login go unresolved? *Because no one owned the problem.*

Solving the root cause of a complex problem like this in our own organization involved many different people across many different departments. When viewed as a customer service problem or an efficiency issue for our customer service team, it was simply impractical organizationally to get traction and investment in resources to address the problem.

Ahh, but when login was viewed as an obstacle to growth with quantifiable impact on member growth, retention, and revenue? That was an entirely different story.

The "login problem" was the genesis of AMA's customer experience program. We called our program "CXOne" to remind the team that if one person took the trouble to contact us about a problem, it was highly likely that many others were experiencing the same issue. It was time to turn our customer listening into action and shift from a customer service "break-fix" model to a more strategic CX transformation model.

***

Building a new capability like CX into an organization is like developing a new muscle. It takes a lot of exercise and fuel. After all, embracing CX is more than introducing a new set of tools and metrics. It's just as much about creating culture change.

From my days as a CDO in the early era of digital transformation, I learned two important things about introducing a new organizational capability:

1. **Don't go around trying to be the visionary**. Instead, talk about how the new capability will power your existing growth initiatives. In those days, that meant talking less about the idea of digital transformation (lofty, vague, expensive) and more about initiatives like search engine optimization, digital content development, and digital marketing. Once those and many other efforts are in place and producing results, then it's okay to look back and talk about your digital transformation!

2. **When starting something transformative, focus initially on a series of small wins that build organizational understanding of your strategy.** Seeing is believing. Over time, these small wins build big momentum that eventually leads to transformation-level success.

So, when it came to AMA's CX approach, we decided to use a similar playbook. We didn't start by trumpeting the big idea of CX. Like throwing around the words "digital transformation," no one would really understand what that was anyway. Instead, we started by identifying and prioritizing the close-in problems that vexed our customers. We put together small, but influential cross-functional teams with the mindset and ability to fix the root causes of customer issues for good. Once that foundation was laid, we broadened our approach by offering similar assistance to other groups across the organization. This resulted in a hybrid approach, with a CX team both embedded in our marketing operation and operating as an enterprise-level CX Center of Excellence that collaborated with different business teams across the organization.

As part of building our CX foundation, we also needed to lay out an explicit CX strategy. In that regard, I made one of my best managerial decisions: Repositioning AMA's Customer Service Leader, Gloria Gupta, as our CX leader. She became our unofficial Chief Friction-Reduction Officer, with an objective to build a program that reflected industry best practices in strategy, customer listening, metrics, and program adoption. Already a long-time, proven customer service leader, she went back to school and completed all four Forrester CX certification programs, met with industry thought leaders and connected with the leading professional and benchmarking organizations. As part of her certification process, we defined the elements of our CX strategy in a formal way, articulated the set of metrics that we would use to measure our success, and identified the tool set that would be crucial to our success, such as journey mapping and customer blueprints.

One of the advantages of building a program from the ground up is that you're not saddled with legacy measures, structures, or old mindsets. For us, it meant starting at the right place, which was tying our customer experience strategy directly to our brand strategy. To use the words of CX guru Jeanne Bliss, that's what CX should help you do – deliver your brand promise.

But surprisingly, I hadn't seen many examples of that because CX strategy is often bolted on organizationally and strategically, like an arm on Frankenstein's monster. At a conference several years ago, I asked a CX executive from a well-known organization with a large and standalone CX unit about their strategy. I was surprised that their CX strategy was separate and distinct from their brand strategy. And I was puzzled by the focus of the conference presentation: A CX initiative focused solely on what type of package should be sent to onboard new members. Don't get me wrong, new member onboarding is important, and this is a valid issue to explore. But I'd consider this more of a membership or marketing initiative, not a separate CX initiative. I could only imagine how this was playing out practically in an organization where teams and leaders are vying for investment, and there is always a challenge coordinating messaging. Separating marketing and CX in this context was bound to lead to territorial skirmishes and questions around funding and prioritization. I wasn't surprised to hear several years later that this team was reorganized.

To me, aligning the AMA CX strategy and brand strategy was essential. But brand strategy is not necessarily second nature in the nonprofit world, where the mission is the more common foundation. Nor is it necessarily second nature in the digital world, where the product is expected to sell itself.

It turned out the timing worked to our advantage in getting the alignment we wanted. We'd only recently refined our brand strategy, "Physicians' Powerful Ally in Patient Care." So, it made sense to use this statement as the North Star for our CX strategy. Our CX objective was quite simple: Remove barriers to delivering our brand promise to physicians. Viewed in that context, we mapped out the membership journey of physicians, identifying the key obstacles at each stage to joining, enjoying membership benefits, and engaging with our products. In partnership with all key X stakeholders on our team – marketing, product, commerce, and service – we identified and prioritized together which CX initiatives would have the biggest impact on growth.

In addition to starting with a focus on delivering our brand promise, building our CX strategy from scratch gave us the opportunity to define the kind of metrics that would be most meaningful and actionable. Unlike many large companies, we didn't have an established trend of Net Promoter Score measures to work from, which in AMA's case, worked in our favor.

***

Net Promoter Score, or NPS, gained prominence in the early 2000s as a benchmark measure of customer loyalty. Derived from a basic question, "Would you recommend this company/product to a friend?" Net Promoter Score divides customers into "promoters," "passives," and "detractors," and calculates an overall score – promoters minus detractors. Tracked over time, Net Promoter Score can provide an important, simple benchmark for companies that is comparable across industries.[1]

There are a lot of companies that are rightfully very proud of their Net Promoter Scores. Some even include their scores in marketing and advertising. But while Net Promoter Scores can provide a customer-centric trend of feelings, it's not necessarily a clear indicator of growth, nor does it necessarily provide actionable

---

[1] Available from: https://hbr.org/2021/11/net-promoter-3-0 [Accessed 13 February 2024].

insight into what's going wrong and how to fix it. That direction requires additional research, which may or may not happen.

Instead of trying to adopt this big-company model, we chose a path that was more appropriate and actionable for us. We needed measurements that showed us specific points of customer friction and let us track how we were doing over time to reduce them. After a lot of research and exploration, we landed on four specific measurements: Customer Effort Score (CES), Customer Friction Index (CXI), First Contact Resolution, and Channel Switching.

Customer Effort Score

The Customer Effort Score was developed in 2010 by the Corporate Executive Board, now Gartner. The concept couldn't be simpler: When you've addressed a customer problem, follow up with a quick survey asking the customer how easy it was for them to get their problem fixed, usually from 1 (very hard) to 7 (very easy). This measure became standard for our customer service team. We chose to use Customer Effort Score instead of Net Promoter Score because we felt like it was more actionable for our organization.

You can read a lot more about the Customer Effort Score and its role in the "Customer Experience Ecosystem" section in the book *Outside In: The Power of Putting Customers at the Center of Your Business* by Harley Manning and Kerry Bodine.

Customer Friction Index

The Customer Friction Index, on the other hand, measures the friction that customers are experiencing when trying to use a certain digital product. This could be an issue with the website or trouble logging in to their membership account. This isn't a rocket science approach. We calculate the Customer Friction Index by dividing the total number of reported problems by the total amount of usage (e.g., sessions or page views). In Phase 1 of this effort, the numerator (reported problems) was generated from the number of email or phone contacts to our customer service team. The denominator (usage) was readily available through our website traffic analytics.

We created our initial set of focus areas and started benchmarking. We tracked friction scores over time as we made incremental product improvements. We aggregated results on a dashboard and shared it with all the business owners and product leaders involved in customer experience across the organization. This approach, which was relatively simple and inexpensive, gave us a data-driven report card for how different initiatives and product improvements reduced friction at key engagement and buying points in the customer journey. The impact of this "friction removal" could be readily translated to ROI.

Using Customer Friction Indices, we prioritized our CX problems and initiated efforts to address them.

Now, here's where a bit more of the rocket science, or at least rocket technology, added some additional friction-reducing power. In Phase 2 of the Customer Friction Index initiative, we used technology to help automate and supplement the manual collection of the friction score numerator – reported problems. This technology, implemented across multiple parts of our website and applications, flagged behavior that indicated a customer problem, such as a broken link or page. Using this automated approach meant we didn't have to rely solely on customers to report the problems themselves. The software did it for us. The only downside: Suddenly, the number of "reported" problems skyrocketed, which was a bit dispiriting. Better to know though, right?

Beyond the benefit of automating the collection of problems we might have otherwise missed, the new software alerted us to concerning trend changes and helped us diagnose what was going wrong. Heat maps pointed out key areas of interaction on the pages in question and indicated possible sources of friction. One of my favorite names for the kind of problem software like this can identify is nicknamed a "rage click." A rage click is the equivalent of when you hit the elevator button a million times to make it arrive faster. On a website, it's where a user clicks repeatedly on a link or button, but nothing happens. As an example, we noticed many "rage clicks" on a particularly important page on our website. When we looked carefully at the heat map, it became obvious that our users were trying to click on an image. But the only actionable part of the image was a small CTA button in the bottom corner. We fixed this annoying friction point immediately by expanding the clickable area to include the entire graphic.

First Contact Resolution and Channel Switching

These CX measures quantify the friction customers experience in resolving problems. The aim: A customer should have their problem resolved on their first attempt without follow-up contacts (first contact resolution) and not have to switch from one approach (e.g., online help or email) to another (e.g., a phone call). The introduction of online chat has been instrumental in reducing channel switching for the AMA, as our customer service agents are often able to resolve customer concerns during a transaction, without any additional follow-up.

Over time, we have been able to create trend lines for all major aspects of the customer journey across many product lines. In most cases, our efforts have led to continuous declines in our friction scores. Through myriad incremental changes that addressed the root causes of customer friction, we've been able to substantially reduce the in-bound contact volume to our service center. And by reducing call volume, we've been able to redeploy resources to root-cause-fixing CX activities and other high-impact initiatives. Talk about a positive cycle!

But the biggest change in our CX program hasn't been just about the technology. Like with so many organizational initiatives, it has been just as much about creating a culture of collaboration around CX. Quite simply, CX was not a term that had previously been part of the organization's lexicon. Like the small wins of digital transformation, progress in defining and improving our customer experience measures has created its own set of momentum and built bridges across our organization as we exported the approach to businesses and divisions outside of membership. Over the past two years, we've created an internal network of nearly 400 stakeholders. In other words, we've enrolled nearly half of the organization as fellow friction fighters, taking our customer experience efforts to an entirely new level. We celebrate the work and accomplishments of all our stakeholders at our annual CX Forum.

As part of connecting with the broader CX community, we've encountered some outstanding CX teams, many at much larger organizations, with far greater resources. But what I hope you take away from our example is that it doesn't take a huge team or millions of dollars to build your CX program and create a band of customer-focused friction fighters. Be scrappy. Use simple, inexpensive measures and build from there, gaining momentum and funding as your wins accumulate.

And know this: It can happen fast. When we started our program, we only wanted to help jumpstart growth, and we certainly did not have any aspirations for recognition. But six years later, our CX program and leadership has won six major U.S. and international awards. My favorite awards went to our CX leader, who was already in her 60s when I asked her to transition to her new role. Two years later, she was named an "Emerging Leader in Customer Experience." A year later, she won a Global Impact Award from a top international CX organization. She's now considered one of the leading practitioners in the CX field and highly sought after for advice.

***

Our approach has been scrappy, and our progress has been incremental and continuous. That doesn't mean we haven't hit some obstacles along the way. You are likely to run into two of the biggest challenges we've contended with: Staffing and organizational structure. How you approach these is very organization-dependent, but here's what we learned.

Staffing

If you're starting a CX operation from scratch, one of the vexing problems is how to get staff and funding for CX initiatives. We solved this issue in three ways.

First, by prioritizing CX, we've managed to gradually shift some headcount out of traditional customer service roles and into CX roles. This is the "positive cycle" I mentioned earlier in the chapter: Shifting from a customer service, "break-fix" model to a CX model can be self-funding. In fact, we've built our CX team without adding any additional headcount to the organization. As our CX initiatives continuously eliminate key underlying causes of friction, we reduce the draw on our customer service team. As a result, we can shift our customer service staff to CX initiatives or other roles without a loss in our service quality.

Second, by creating a culture of CX, we've enlisted an array of CX collaborators across the organization, including many business and product leaders. That takes our CX army from a few people to hundreds. In other words, our role is to lead and coordinate CX initiatives, but nearly all of our friction fighters come from other teams.

Third, because we have chosen to center our CX operation within a broader "X" team, our CX funding needs are included as part of our growth initiatives. From a budgeting standpoint, CX initiatives look more like product and marketing initiatives with defined ROI.

Organizational structure

We chose to build our CX operation within the organizational context of a growth-oriented team of marketers and product developers. We structured it this way to achieve X-level teamwork, with marketing, product, commerce, and service all operating in alignment. Where CX best fits in your organization might be different. There are a number of different options:

- A standalone CX unit

- In Marketing

- In Operations (e.g., IT or Customer Service)

- As an enterprise "Center of Excellence" resource

- An "Office of the CXO" senior-level role

There are advantages and disadvantages to each option, and I've seen some pretty heated arguments on LinkedIn about which approach works best. Again, what works for your organization may be different than ours, but I'll give you a few good reasons why our hybrid model, a Center of Excellence that's part of the X team, works well for us.

First, our customer service center was already serving an enterprise resource, and we had established relationships across the organization. Expanding our offering to include CX support was both intuitive and evolutionary. It was kind of like adding dinner to a restaurant that previously had only served breakfast and lunch. Our job was to engage the organization with this new set of services, which we did through pilot programs.

Second, there are many benefits to aligning CX directly with the four X corners we've discussed: Marketing, product, commerce, and service. These benefits include team alignment, prioritization, and funding.

Third, seating CX alongside marketing has specific benefits for these organizational soulmates. The marketing team is strong at storytelling, amplifying data, and putting voice-of-the-customer learning into action. The CX team is essential to identifying and eliminating friction points that choke growth.

From a practical standpoint, using a Center of Excellence model creates a win–win for the organization, especially in situations we discussed earlier where nobody "owns" the problem. Here's an example: We recently undertook an initiative to increase usage of an online learning platform for resident physicians. While this "product" was part of my team's responsibilities, it involved many different groups. It became clear that we needed to take a system-level view of all the friction points, from start to finish. We parachuted the CX team in to lead the charge. One of my very proud moments recently was walking into the room and seeing a cross-functional team with a customer blueprint diagram that was bigger than I am. The team had mapped out the entire customer experience in detail, identified the friction points, and had already begun prioritizing initiatives.

Excited to see the gigantic customer blueprint our AMA CX team prepared to identify key points of friction with our online learning platform.

***

Hopefully, this chapter provides a clear understanding of the discipline of CX and its role in reducing customer friction. The AMA's scrappy example is proof that you don't need to work in a mega-corporation or spend a ton of money to build your CX practice. The results are measurable and tied directly to customer growth and engagement.

Like in so many areas of business, CX technology is moving rapidly. Automating our friction-collection efforts at the AMA are already having a big impact. Imagine what the future holds as AI, automation, and analytics platforms begin to converge.

A big part of the CXO's role is adapting to – and incorporating – new technology in pursuit of reducing customer friction. The future is not about (also) being a technology expert. It's about having the right outlook and approach, regardless of whatever technology arises. Time to dream big. Is a friction-free customer experience on the horizon? Let's take a look.

The journey ahead

Chapter 10
The friction-free future

Earlier in the book, I talked about navigating the rapid progression of the digital media storytelling platform, all of which occurred over a relatively short period of time. If you're operating in the digital world, you get used to and thrive on an incredibly fast pace of change. It's inevitable. And it is one of the reasons I don't panic when I think about AI; innovations like ChatGPT or the rise of the latest social media platform. Not to discount the momentousness of any of these innovations, but I've seen this movie before. At least this far in my career, innovations like these have always translated to more capabilities and growth opportunities.

The same will be true with the 10-second customer journey. I'm not sure how to describe a faster-moving tornado funnel, but I imagine there will be an opportunity to come up with a sequel to this book – maybe "The 5-Second Customer Journey?" Not to be overly dramatic, but with new tools, technology, and approaches on the horizon, many incorporating AI, we could be looking at the end of friction as we know it.

What does a friction-free future look like?

- Talking to the right people, in the right way, at the right time.
- Flawless handoffs all the way through the funnel.
- Consistent performance across all channels.
- Data to show what worked and didn't work to drive growth.
- The ability to predict and prevent service failures before they happen.
- Retention mechanisms that preserve your relationship and customer loyalty.

This is not futuristic stuff. A lot of technology to support this vision is already here and in use, from ad targeting to marketing automation systems to voice-of-the-customer software to loyalty programs. It's just that, in its current form, it is sometimes manual to operate and often disconnected.

To put these and future technologies to use, it is a given that the CXOs of tomorrow are going to need to be different from the CXOs of today. In addition to being good at what we've discussed in this book, they will need to play a key role in defining the CX Tech Stack of the Future, a collection of technologies that minimizes friction – perhaps to zero – and maximizes growth and retention. While AI innovations dominate the news right now, there will always be a flow of new technology that changes both customer capabilities and experience, just as there have been for decades. Even more importantly, the CXO will need to be a leader in collecting, employing, and acting on data, which will be the fuel for the future of CX, whatever new technologies emerge. Simply put, it will be impossible to master the tornado funnel without expert-level integration of data into its every step.

The CXO of the future will test and leverage these new technologies appropriately to drive growth. And just like I've witnessed an array of innovations across digital media platforms, I've seen a lot of different technologies come and go over the past

20 years. It's wise to be very thoughtful about what new tools you take on because it's not just about a tool or technology. There's the time it takes to set it up, to use it, to analyze its effectiveness, and to sustain interest in that piece of technology as a growth driver. That's way harder than it sounds and involves tremendous resources.

Tools and technologies change. What won't ever get outdated? Having the right mentality and approaches to responding to change. I call these my "five As for creating a friction-free future:"

1. **Automate**: The most useful technologies of the future will do what the most useful technologies of the past have done: Replace key manual activities and inputs with automated processes. Surviving the tornado funnel is easier if you have automation to do as much as possible for you. Let's look at a few examples of this.

   In the last chapter on CX, I talked about how we outfitted our entire website with software that automatically flags and reports suspected CX problems. By monitoring specific user behaviors or outcomes, we can identify friction behaviors like "rage clicks." Right now, we look at dashboards regularly to check for aberrations, or use the tool to help us figure out why performance might be down in a certain area. But in the not-too-distant future, we will not even need to wait. These issues will be reported in real time against benchmarks, and any aberration will trigger an automatic alert, possibly accompanied by diagnostics that indicate where the problem might be. Technology will allow us to automate the process, save precious time (and lost sales) without constant human vigilance on the data collection process. What a relief it is not to worry about finding out our sign-up process is broken for hours before anyone notices – now we get an automated alert right away.

2. **Augment**: There is massive interest in experimentation with generative AI, owing to the advent of large language models like ChatGPT. There also is great concern about the impact of this technology on jobs, including many of those employed in marketing, as the technology shows great promise in content creation, editing, even marketing plan development. Even though I work in an environment where our content must be 100% hallucination-free – free of the incorrect information we've seen generated by AI – these capabilities are important to explore.

Similarly, there is a lot of talk about AI in medicine and concerns about how it could be leveraged by both physicians and patients. Even at present, there are concerns about people self-diagnosing their medical conditions after consulting "Dr. Google." So, one can imagine where this scenario could go seriously awry with even more sophisticated AI tools, which may or may not be "hallucination-free." Similar to the discussion in many other professions, there are also natural concerns about AI "replacing" physicians.

Given the stakes, the current outlook is not about replacing physicians, but using AI to augment their capabilities. For example, AI can be leveraged to identify a microscopic issue on a scan that a human eye might overlook. Or AI could alleviate ongoing obstacles physicians face every day, like taking notes in their electronic health record system or responding to the overwhelming number of messages coming through patient portals. Leveraging AI to address the low value, mundane (and burnout-inducing) tasks could mean a chance to spend more time with patients.

Once we get through the hysteria of the current moment, we're likely to see a similar outcome across the CX spectrum – with AI augmenting our ability to optimize the "right audience, right message, right time" aspect of our marketing. Many of these capabilities are already being built in as features in existing marketing automation systems. For instance, we're using the AI capabilities of our marketing automation engine to determine personalized approaches to email. Our platform helps us figure out what email to send to what person at what time. This has allowed us to reduce email messaging frequency and unsubscribe rates without sacrificing engagement and conversion.

3. **Analyze and Act**: One of the first uses of AI I encountered was at the *Daily Racing Form*. We had launched a betting platform and were eager to increase the number of wagering customers and their betting amount in a very competitive environment. At a conference, I came across a company that was already using AI software in the gaming industry to track, analyze, and predict patterns among casino gamblers. The capabilities of the system were amazing. With such huge amounts of data and frequent transactions, they could identify behavioral patterns from the moment of sign-up and provide appropriate incentives to increase engagement and retention.

For instance, many sports gaming companies use special offers like "Bet $10 and get $20 in free bets" to entice new customers. Not surprisingly, getting a new customer to take advantage of the offer within a limited time frame is a major predictor of retention and churn. So, gaming companies design promotional campaigns targeting these customers to encourage them to act. The same AI software can detect when a customer's betting patterns have slowed, indicating they may be using another platform or are about to churn – meaning leaving one platform for another. To avoid that, companies build automated promotional plans that kick in as soon as a suspected behavioral pattern emerges. The ROI on approaches that re-engage customers like this is well known and easy to measure.

While this AI-driven approach has been used in gaming for many years, the same concepts are just now making their way into non-gaming businesses. AI-based software detects behavioral patterns and allows organizations to create personalized campaigns for many different segments to improve customer retention.

Many B2B companies already use scoring approaches to identify and classify high-potential prospects. Similar mechanisms allow B2C companies to connect content and marketing efforts to create customer engagement scores, which can be used in targeted marketing and retention campaigns.

4. **Align**: Technology itself is only part of a solution. No matter what the latest and greatest innovation brings, true success still is about people and relationships, both internal and external to your organization.

   Internal: This is about alignment with the Chief Information Officer/Chief Technology Officer and other key groups in the organization. Given the emphasis on data, these folks should be some of a CXO's closest colleagues in the organization, as they are best prepared to help them think at an enterprise level about what and how to deploy.

   External: You can't do this on your own. You need to surround yourself with a network of growth-oriented vendors and partners who will bring you along. For example, Salesforce, a company which develops customer relationship management and marketing automation software, is already incorporating AI capabilities into their products. Because Salesforce works with so many customers, it has extensive learning about what is working for companies in a range of industries. It's easier to work with one company than create a CX tech smorgasbord with a lot of separate companies. Partnering with growth-oriented marketing agencies with proven track records of success is another valuable external connection. Vokal, a growth-oriented development agency in Chicago, has been an essential partner in the AMA's digital transformation over the past five years.

There you have it. The five As to driving the future of customer experience: Automate. Augment. Analyze and Act. Align.

Having this mindset helps you synthesize the myriad technological options and approaches that seem to be coming like a firehose these days. And it makes you open to new solutions you otherwise might have missed. How could technology help someone like a CXO achieve the vision of a friction-free future? An answer came unexpectedly to me, and it involved hot dogs.

***

I am not a baseball fan. So, an invitation to an advertiser-sponsored rooftop event to watch a Chicago Cubs game is not really my thing. But this invitation came out of the blue from Brian Cahak, the consultant I worked with on A/B testing at the *Daily Racing Form*. He wanted to catch up and tell me about his new venture in the world of event-based analytics.

I remembered the advice of one of our former AMA Presidents, Dr. Gerald Harmon, who once told me, "It's a small world if you make it that way." In that "make it a small world" spirit, I overcame my baseball aversion and took Brian up on his invitation, and I'm so glad I did. While the game was playing out, Brian gave me a firehose introduction to event-based analytics. And along with a couple of hot dogs, I got a huge helping of how event-based analytics will help transform the future of customer experience.

To put it simply, event-based analytics is a technology that allows you to track and analyze interactions between customers and your product. Each individual interaction constitutes an event, whether it is opening an email or clicking a link in a social media post. And these actions are tracked across every digital touchpoint such as mobile apps, email, or a website.

As customers trigger events through their interactions with your digital platform, their behaviors and other attributes are recorded, along with other information you might have access to, such as their location, the device they are on, their email address, or their mobile phone number. Add all this information together and you have a treasure trove of data to analyze and act upon.

For me, event-based analytics is like what would happen if A/B testing and predictive gaming software got together and had a data baby.

The first thing I discovered in my rapid-fire conversation with Brian was that he, too, was thinking about the "X" factor in customer experience. From his angle, the opportunity was to bring together the separate streams of product, marketing, commerce, and customer analytics data and connect them to marketing activation platforms. That vision resonated with my five As approach to the future: Automate. Augment. Analyze and Act. Align.

It also made me think back to the vision of the one-to-one marketing future that Don Peppers and Martha Rogers proposed nearly 30 years ago. Essentially, they recommended identifying your best user segments and using technology to communicate with them in a more personalized way. But how that could be accomplished was limited by the technology of the era. Enter AI and marketing automation, and the five As begin to work together to bring the dream to fruition.

Advances in technology will help drive customer experience by connecting and automating the four underlying components. Think about how the key parts of the playbook can be knitted together, end-to-end. Embraced by a test-and-learn culture, platforms that automate the collection of key data points, analyze and benchmark against key metrics, identify friction, and execute segment-based marketing plans will offer powerful competitive advantages to those who know how to leverage the technology.

It's similar to how AI will augment physicians and free them from some of the mundane and frustrating tasks that take time away from patient care. In the same way, AI will free marketers up to spend more time thinking about their customers.

***

As we head into the home stretch of this book (you can take the CXO out of horse racing, but you can't take the horse racing out of the CXO), we could spend a lot of time postulating what the future of CX *could* be. Perhaps we'll nail 40% or 50% of what actually *will* be – if we're lucky. Mention the tornado funnel to a marketing person in the 1950s and they would have thought you were talking about *The Wizard of Oz*. No one in the 1980s imagined the internet would make the world so much smaller and so much more complex at the same time. And who could have predicted that mobile phones would morph into web-surfing supercomputers in our pockets?

I can't say with any degree of certainty what specific pieces of technology will make the biggest difference in the life of the CXO of the future. What I can say is this: If the CXOs of the present don't master the 10-second customer journey right now, they won't be around to play a major role in shaping the field's future.

The other guarantee I can make is that CXOs can't do this alone.

Chapter 11

Bringing it all together, together

I started the book talking about my first experience with the 10-second customer journey while I was planning a family trip to Paris. I'll finish with one final lesson inspired by a somewhat different journey – a classic road trip from my younger days.

During my senior year in college, a group of buddies and I made the 14-hour spring break drive from Ohio to Florida. My fellow passengers wanted to make a pact: If any driver got a speeding ticket, we would all pitch in for the cost. Now, I barely had enough money to be going to Florida in the first place, so I was uncomfortable with this arrangement. While we had a common destination in mind, we were not necessarily in sync about how the trip should go down – how fast we would drive, where we would stop, or how we would manage the long overnight (and sometimes sleepy) driving responsibilities. I didn't know some of the guys in the car very well. The last thing I wanted or could afford was being on the hook for hundreds of dollars in fines because my fellow drivers were speeding down I-75 at 95 mph.

In other words, we didn't have a clear understanding of the collaboration model for a seamless journey.

That's the same with many organizations today. I've been fortunate to work in several organizations where I had a reasonable span of control over the elements of customer experience, but this is not the norm or reality for most people. And, unless you're a CEO (something I've never been), there are always many parts of any business or organization that don't report to you, share your goals and incentives, or align with your priorities.

The key to building the 10-second customer journey in today's environment is a skill that I referred to throughout the playbook, at least implicitly. So, let's make this skill explicit: Collaboration.

You might recall in Chapter 1 that I was surprised to find "being collaborative with other executives" as one of the CXO job *responsibilities*. In retrospect, I'd describe it as a job *requirement*.

Breaking down the silos of companies large and small requires more than surface levels of collaboration. This is not about collaboration for collaboration's sake. It's about *meaningful* collaboration. In his book, *Collaboration: How Leaders Avoid the Traps, Create Unity, and Reap Big Results*, Morten Hansen lays out a convincing framework for evaluating collaboration opportunities and determining their value. Hansen recounts a story about one of my personal business heroes, A.G. Lafley, the former Chairman and CEO of my first employer, P&G. The brand management structure that I encountered at P&G in the 1980s taught me a lot about how to orchestrate customer experience, but even an organization like that can go off the rails under the pressures of constant innovation and technological development. Lafley's clearly articulated vision and dedication to what Hansen calls "disciplined collaboration" righted the ship. Not surprisingly, this kind of collaboration required dynamic teamwork across marketing, product, commerce, and service. And for P&G, it created billions of dollars of value.

You might have read through the ideas in the 10-second customer journey, with its emphasis on the seamless marketing-product-commerce-service model, and thought it was naïve given the structures that most people work within today. I get it. So, is the 10-second customer journey just some kind of utopian vision?

There are three reasons to be optimistic that the 10-second customer journey vision will translate to reality.

First, moving as fast as the customer moves is a business imperative. New companies with the hang of the 10-second customer journey are emerging all the time, challenging giant organizations to become not only more digitally enabled, but also more seamless in their delivery of customer experience.

Second is the developing discipline of CX. The folks being trained in this discipline bring a special skill set, tools, metrics, and collaborative approach to obliterate friction and unlock growth. Perhaps most importantly, they can operate in the "unowned" spaces that sit between the steps of the customer journey. As organizations become more familiar with the value of CX, I think we'll see CX leaders become key players in company growth engines.

Third, as we discussed in the last chapter, AI will eliminate some of the heavy lifting for CXOs, meaning new technology will make the 10-second customer journey easier to achieve. Just like you rarely worry about your car engine overheating on a trip or getting lost, new platforms, powered by AI, will eliminate some of the heavy lifting.

***

We hear a lot these days about creating a customer-centric *culture*. But we don't necessarily hear a lot about creating a customer-centric organizational *structure* or *leadership*. Why? Because re-organizing around customer needs – and finding the right leaders – means more than just talk or merely swapping out one C-level leader for another. The traditional walls between marketing, product, commerce, and service directly create the friction that prevents the 10-second customer journey. Leaders who can bring together the pillars of the X will undoubtedly be even more essential in the future. Whether that "X" leader is called a Chief Experience Officer, Chief Marketing Officer, or Chief Growth Officer isn't the point. But someone needs to take on the role.

Whatever the X leader is called, the North Star remains the same: Eliminate friction to move customers through the tornado funnel in ten seconds. Hopefully, my playbook has given you some insight into exactly how to pull that off. In the spirit of moving as quickly as the tornado funnel, here's a 10-second version of the CXO's playbook to guide your efforts:

1. Use data and insight to identify an actionable target customer definition.

2. Develop a brand proposition so compelling and insightful that it gets The Nod in a few seconds.

3. Create a well-packaged product that brings the brand proposition to life.

4. Build a 6-S storytelling platform that supports a results-driven "binge marketing" plan.

5. Make checkout a snap with friction-free commerce.

6. Here is the foundation to support the steps of this approach:

   a. A test-and-learn culture that generates (and celebrates) constant learning and improvement.
   b. CX capabilities that predict and eliminate the root causes of friction.
   c. Thoughtful incorporation of new friction-reduction technologies.

d. Meaningful team collaboration centered around growth and results.

I hope that seeing this short list of steps and points doesn't make you regret having read all the way through the book instead of skipping right to the end. But I do hope that the playbook will allow you to skip past some of the mistakes I've made along the way. Perhaps it will save you some time as you envision the changes that need to happen in your own organization. It would make me feel great to know that someone, somewhere, made a copy of this list and tacked it on their wall to remind them that there can be a better way.

Thank you for taking this journey with me. We've covered a lot of ground. I hope you have picked up some useful knowledge and enjoyed the stories I told along the way. With the playbook as your guide, it's time for you to start building a friction-free experience for your customers. In this case, the destination is the 10-second customer journey.

I can't wait to see what you create.

Recommended reading

For those who would like to learn more about the world of customer experience and navigating the 10-second customer journey, I enlisted the AMA's globally recognized CX leader, Gloria Gupta, to assemble a recommended reading list.

Berger, Jonah. *The Catalyst: How to Change Anyone's Mind*. Simon & Schuster, 2022.

Bliss, Jeanne. *Chief Customer Officer 2.0: How to Build Your Customer-Driven Growth Engine*. 2nd Edition, Jossey-Bass, 2015.

Brand, Stewart. *The Clock of the Long Now: Time and Responsibility*. Basic Books, 1999.

Carbone, Lewis P. and Haeckel, Stephan H. "Engineering Customer Experiences" in *Marketing Management*, Vol 3, January 1994.

CXPA Book of Knowledge, 1st Edition, Customer Experience Professionals Association.

Dixon, Matthew, Toman, Nick and Delisi, Rick. *The Effortless Experience: Conquering the New Battleground for Customer Loyalty*. Portfolio Penguin, 2013.

Gothelf, Jef and Seidan, Josh. *Sense and Respond: How Successful Organizations Listen to Customers and Create New Products Continuously.* Harvard Business Review Press, 2017.

Hansen, Morten. *Collaboration: How Leaders Avoid the Traps, Create Unity, and Reap Big Results.* Harvard Business Review Press, 2009.

Heath, Chip and Heath, Dan. *Switch: How to Change Things When Change is Hard.* Random House Business, 2011.

Heath, Chip and Heath, Dan. *The Power of Moments: Why Certain Experiences have Extraordinary Impact.* Bantam Press, 2017.

Heath, Dan. *Upstream: How to Solve Problems Before They Happen.* Bantam Press, 2020.

Huang, Jason and Lai, Michael T. *X Thinking: Building Better Brands in the Age of eXperience.* Forward by B. Joseph Pine II. X Thinking Institute, 2022.

Kalbach, Jim. Mapping Experiences: *A Complete Guide to Creating Value through Journeys, Blueprints, and Diagrams.* O'Reilly Media, 2016.

Manning, Harley and Bodine, Kerry. *Outside In: The Power of Putting Customers at the Center of Your Business.* Amazon Publishing, 2012.

Nordgren, Loran and Schonthal, David. *The Human Element: Overcoming the Resistance that Awaits New Ideas.* Wiley, 2011.

Peppers, Don and Rogers, Martha, PhD. *The One to One Future: Building Relationships One Customer at a Time.* Currency Doubleday, 1997.

Pine II, B. Joseph and Gilmore, James H. *The Experience Economy: Competing for Time, Attention, and Money.* Harvard Business Review Press, 2019.

Ries, Eric. *The Lean Startup.* Portfolio Penguin, 2011.

Rossman, J. Robert and Duerden, Matthew D. *Designing Experiences*. Foreword by B. Joseph Pine II. Columbia University Press, 2019.

Tincher, Jim and Newman, Nicole. *How Hard is it to Be Your Customer? Using Journey Mapping to Drive Customer-Focused Change*. Paramount Market Publishing Inc., 2019.

Acknowledgments

It should come as no surprise that a 10-second customer journey inspired me to write this book.

As part of my New Year's resolutions, I mentioned to my wife for the 100th time that I was thinking about writing a book. She encouragingly responded by sending me a link to a 10-Day Book Proposal Publishing Challenge. The challenge was run by Alison Jones of Practical Inspiration Publishing, whose newsletter my wife reads. Alison, in similar fashion to Blake at GuerrillaZen, has cast a wide digital net with her insightful newsletter and blog.

I decided to sign up for the challenge in less than ten seconds, just for fun. And it was fun. In ten days, I had written all the elements of my book proposal, which I could theoretically present to publishers. I hadn't really thought much about the competition aspect of the challenge though.

Unexpectedly, I won. And with that came a publishing deal from Practical Inspiration Publishing.

Alison and I agreed on a timetable for writing the book, the length, etc. Then, I sat down and began trying to turn my snappy marketing copy into actual chapters. That's when I realized I had no idea what I was doing. Months of staring blankly at my computer passed. Only when I saw the book go up for pre-order online (and friends told me they'd ordered it) did the creative fires start burning. I am deeply grateful to Alison Jones for her continuing encouragement, Alison Gray, a developmental editor, for her thoughtful review, and to Marc Zarefsky and John Agliata, without whose writing assistance this book would still be a disconnected mess.

This book captures wisdom that has been passed down to me by many of my managers/mentors throughout my career. I feel fortunate to have worked with and learned from the best people in marketing, advertising, digital media, and customer experience. I think about the lessons they taught me every day. Thank you, Don Uzzi, Brad Brinegar, Jack Phifer, Doug Holroyd, Donn Davis, Neil Smit, Jim Riesenbach, Tom Beusse, John Hartig, Jordan Goldberg, Jody Swavy, Bernie Hengesbaugh, Rick Tanner, and the many others who gave me so many opportunities to succeed.

I am deeply indebted to those who gave me the generous gift of reading my book draft and providing thoughtful comments. Thank you, Fergus Clare, Dr. James Madara, Jon Giacomin, Chunka Mui, Andra Heller, Joe Thornton, Gloria Gupta, Jeff Phillips, Jef Capaldi, Kevin O'Reilly, Kristen Tinney, Ryan Wells, Zach Frazier, Laurie McGraw, Grant Viola, India Unger-Harquail, Evangeline Unger-Harquail, Brian Unger, Brian Cahak, and Blake Bowman. I am grateful to Kristin Reynolds, Debra Berk, Dan Fox, and Joe Thompson for their design advice and assistance.

Thank you to all my colleagues at the AMA who have been on this journey with me, including Ken Sharigian, Denise Hagerty, and Michael Tutty. Working with my leadership team, the Marketing and Member Experience Team, our Senior Management Group and the AMA Board of Trustees has had a profound impact on me and inspired a good portion of this book. I would never have been in a position to talk about customer experience without the support and leadership of the AMA CX team, led by Gloria Gupta and Jeff Phillips, and the many others who have collaborated with us on AMA's CX initiatives.

Thank you to Norm Yustin and Mindy Kairey for bringing me the life-changing opportunity at AMA.

It is an honor to serve the physicians, resident physicians, and medical students of this nation. I am in awe of them and their commitment to patient care.

Finally, a special thanks to my wife, CV Harquail, who inspired this writing journey and assisted greatly in the writing and editing of the book. An author herself, she understands the process and kept me from giving up. We learned a long time ago in a pre-marriage workshop run by the renowned author Harville Hendrix that enduring love is about supporting each other's growth over a lifetime. I am so fortunate to have her on this journey with me.

Index

About the author

Todd Unger is the Chief Experience Officer of the American Medical Association (AMA), where he has driven record growth and gained international recognition for the AMA's CX program. He is the co-creator and host of *AMA Update*, the organization's award-winning daily video/podcast series, available on the AMA's YouTube channel and on Spotify and Apple Podcasts.

A transformational marketing and digital executive, Unger's experience places him at the nexus of marketing, content, e-commerce, technology, product development, and customer service – the building blocks of today's customer experience.

Unger's career began at marketing and advertising powerhouses Procter & Gamble (P&G) and the Leo Burnett Company. He then leapt into the exploding digital world as a product manager in the early days of America Online and served as General Manager of AOL's local city guide operation, *Digital City*. As a Chief Digital Officer and Chief Marketing Officer, he's led digital marketing, product, and content teams across large and small media companies, including Lifetime Television, Time4 Media (a division of Time, Inc.), and the *Daily Racing Form*.

Unger is a frequent speaker and podcast guest on the topics of marketing and customer experience. He holds an MBA from Harvard Business School. For more information and updates, visit toddunger.com.

A quick word from Practical Inspiration Publishing...

We hope you found this book both practical and inspiring – that's what we aim for with every book we publish.

We publish titles on topics ranging from leadership, entrepreneurship, HR and marketing to self-development and wellbeing.

Find details of all our books at: www.practicalinspiration.com

 Did you know...

We can offer discounts on bulk sales of all our titles - ideal if you want to use them for training purposes, corporate giveaways or simply because you feel these ideas deserve to be shared with your network.

We can even produce bespoke versions of our books, for example with your organization's logo and/or a tailored foreword.

To discuss further, contact us on info@practicalinspiration.com.

 Got an idea for a business book?

We may be able to help. Find out more about publishing in partnership with us at: bit.ly/PIpublishing.

Follow us on social media...

@PIPTalking

@pip_talking

@practicalinspiration

@piptalking

Practical Inspiration Publishing